Gresley A4s

The LNER's Streamlined Pacific Locomotives

Gavin Morrison

Ian Allan
PUBLISHING

Front cover: No 60017 *Silver Fox* waiting to take over an up express for Kings Cross just outside Doncaster at the south end on 29 April 1962. *Gavin Morrison*

Back cover: No 60007 *Sir Nigel Gresley* in BR blue livery crosses Summerseat Viaduct on the East Lancashire Railway with a morning train for Ramsbottom on 24 January 1998. *Gavin Morrison*

Title page: Quicksilver in its final condition heading an up Newcastle express past Stukeley, north of Huntingdon, on 11 September 1959. Until their final few years, members of the class were seldom seen off their regular diagram, but on 20 February 1954 *Quicksilver* hauled a football special from King's Cross to Crook, and was piloted from Darlington by a Class A8 4-6-2T. *E. R. Wethersett / Ian Allan Library*

Contents

Bibliography

LNER Locomotives Part 2A & 11— Railway Correspondence & Travel Society.
The 'A4' Pacifics — P. N. Townend, Ian Allan Publishing

First published 2001

ISBN 0 7110 2725 0

Published by Ian Allan Publishing

an imprint of Ian Allan Publishing Ltd, Terminal House, Shepperton, Surrey TW17 8AS.
Printed by Ian Allan Printing Ltd, Riverdene Business Park, Hersham, Surrey KT12 4RG.

Code: 0201/B1

Introduction

It was a sunny August morning in 1953 and, as the train from King's Cross slowed for its stop at Stevenage, a railway-mad ten-year-old peered out of the window. Rapidly approaching was the wedge-shaped front of a locomotive type he had never seen before, yet immediately recognised. In a blur of shiny green and polished steel, 'A4' Pacific No 60009 *Union of South Africa* swept past, followed by a rake of immaculate crimson and cream carriages. The sight, sound and smell was over in an instant — but I was hooked!

In the months leading up to my family's move from South London to the new town of Stevenage I had been eagerly looking forward to this moment. I was not disappointed. The train I had just seen was the 9am to Edinburgh — the Saturday working of one of the two locomotives and sets of stock which, on Mondays to Fridays, formed the non-stop 'Elizabethan'. Later I was to appreciate the significance of the fact that my first 'A4' was one of the Haymarket-based examples, normally seen at the south end of the East Coast main line only during the summer months.

Many people remember vividly their first sight of an 'A4' — and that must certainly have applied to those who were around when they first appeared. Gresley's development of the 'A3', the 'A4' was designed to power a new LNER lightweight high-speed service between London and Newcastle, the 'Silver Jubilee', introduced in the autumn of 1935. In the fashion of the 1930s, the locomotive and train were streamlined, and the appearance of the first of the new Pacifics, No 2509 *Silver Link*, was little short of sensational. Both its shape and the silver-grey colour scheme were like nothing seen in Britain before.

How much the streamlining contributed to performance is now generally accepted as minimal, wind resistance being reduced to any degree only at the highest speeds. That high speeds could be reached was amply demonstrated just two weeks after *Silver Link* had run light engine from Doncaster to King's Cross on 13 September 1935 and worked a stopping train to Cambridge next morning. On the public trial run of the 'Silver Jubilee' on 27 September, *Silver Link* ran the 105½ miles from King's Cross to Grantham and back with the seven-coach train. A speed of 112½mph was reached twice on the northbound run, at Arlesey and again at Sandy, in both

cases on almost-level track. For 25 consecutive miles the train ran at 100mph or more, and the whole journey was completed in 88 minutes, averaging more than 71mph from start to stop.

Entering service three days later, the 'Silver Jubilee' was not required to run at such high speeds, but its four-hour schedule, including stops, nevertheless represented an overall average speed of 67mph. *Silver Link* itself worked the train single-handed, making a return trip five days a week for two weeks until the second 'A4' was ready. It was a remarkable debut for the class.

Over the next three years, the four silver engines designated for this train were joined by another 31, the first few in the standard LNER apple green colour scheme for general use. The 'silver' names of the first four were joined by names of birds described as being 'noted for their swift or powerful flight'. Perhaps that description is questionable as far as some of the birds are concerned, but it was certainly appropriate for the locomotives. Garter blue livery was applied to seven new 'A4s' allocated to work two more 'streamliners' introduced in 1937. For the 'Coronation', five of these engines were named after countries of what was then the British Empire, while the two designated to work the 'West Riding Limited' were given names considered appropriate to the wool industry — *Golden Fleece* and *Golden Shuttle*.

After a final few 'A4s' were completed in the standard green livery, blue was adopted for the remaining engines. These included the 100th Gresley Pacific, which entered service in November 1937 as the first 'A4' to carry the name of an individual — No 4498 *Sir Nigel Gresley*. Earlier examples were similarly repainted by the end of 1938.

Of the three high-speed trains, the 'Coronation' was the most demanding, its six-hour timing between London and Edinburgh only equalled when the 'Deltic'-hauled expresses were accelerated in 1962. Although the 'Coronation' stopped *en route*, the same locomotive worked the train throughout its journey.

Another through working between the two capital cities was on the 'Flying Scotsman', which, since 1928, had been running non-stop in the summer months. In 1937, 'A4s' took over this duty from the earlier Gresley Pacifics and the schedule was cut by 15 minutes, to 7 hours. The engines employed on this

working were those with corridor tenders, 10 of them dating from 1928 and transferred from the unstreamlined Pacifics, plus another 11 built with the 'A4s'. The last 14 'A4s' entered service between November 1937 and July 1938 with non-corridor tenders. The number of corridor-fitted 'A4s' increased by one in 1948 when the tender from Class W1 No 60700 was attached to No 60004 *William Whitelaw* and remained with this locomotive to the end.

Towards the end of the construction run, No 4468 *Mallard* was built in March 1938 with a double Kylchap chimney. The last three members of the class were similarly equipped. It was *Mallard*, of course, which achieved the greatest fame of all, for its unbeaten world speed record for steam of 126mph, attained during the descent from Stoke Summit with a test train on 3 July 1938. Together with their consistent performance on the streamlined trains, the 'A4s' were thus at the forefront of high-speed rail travel.

It came to an end abruptly with the outbreak of World War 2 at the beginning of September 1939. The three 'streamliners' made their final runs on 31 August, the summer non-stop operation of the 'Flying Scotsman' ceased and schedules were eased on the East Coast main line. For a while, even, the King's Cross 'A4s' were put into store.

During the war years the 'A4s' were called upon to haul trains of prodigious weight, far in excess of those for which they were intended. On one occasion, *Silver Link* worked from King's Cross to Newcastle with a train of 25 vehicles — three times the weight of the 'Silver Jubilee'. Another 'A4' was clocked at 78mph on the Darlington-York 'racing' stretch with 22 coaches behind the tender. To avoid confusion with air-raid sirens, the chime whistles were replaced by standard whistles and, for ease of maintenance, the valances covering the wheels were removed. Chime whistles (although not the originals) were restored after the war but the valances were not.

Renaming of some 'A4s' after directors and officers of the LNER had begun in the early months of 1939 and continued during the war. One of the renamed engines, No 4469 *Sir Ralph Wedgwood* (formerly *Gadwall*) was damaged beyond repair in an air raid on York at the end of April 1942 and was withdrawn two months later. New nameplates were cast and, in January 1944, the name was transferred to No 4466, formerly *Herring Gull*. One of the original *Sir Ralph Wedgwood* nameplates has recently come to light after spending more than half a century in a garden shed.

Inevitably, years of neglect took their toll, and the 'A4s' ended the war with their wartime black livery hidden under layers of grime and their boiler casings disfigured by dents. The LNER renumbering scheme of 1946 originally allocated the numbers 580-613 to the 'A4s', in order of construction. This was revised after only four were renumbered, and the numbers 1-34 were allocated instead. For prestige reasons, those already carrying the names of LNER directors and officers were placed first, followed by *Dwight D. Eisenhower* and the five 'Coronation' engines. The rest of the order was determined in order of their running numbers, rather than by order of construction as the renumbering scheme intended. However, the last two built — No 4902 *Seagull* and No 4903 *Peregrine* (which was to become *Lord Faringdon* in 1948) — at least took the numbers 33 and 34 respectively.

A keenness to return to high-speed running was evidenced in May 1946 when *Silver Fox* ran from King's Cross to Edinburgh and back with a test train. Speed restrictions were lifted for the occasion, and the 'A4' achieved 102mph down Stoke Bank on the return journey.

While the prewar history of the 'A4s' was dominated by their use on the streamlined trains, their career after the war was no less interesting. In the matter of liveries, a reversion to Garter blue was quickly put in hand by the LNER, and all were so treated by March 1948, just after Nationalisation. That summer saw four members of the class repainted in an experimental livery, usually described as purple. In common with the main express-passenger classes of the other 'Big Four' companies, the 'A4s' then received a dark blue livery in 1949/50 before the standard BR green was applied, from August 1951 onwards.

The year 1948 was a notable one in the career of the class, for more than one reason. It was, of course, the year of Nationalisation, when a further renumbering gave the 'A4s' their final identities as Nos 60001-34. For the 'Locomotive Exchanges' in May and June, the Eastern Region selected double-chimney engines to take part in the comparative trials with locomotives of the other 'Big Four' companies. *Seagull* acquitted itself well on the former Southern and Great Western main lines to the West of England, as did *Lord Faringdon* on the West Coast route.

Non-stop summer operation of the 'Flying Scotsman' was reintroduced in June 1948, but lasted for just one season. During that summer, an unexpected record was achieved by

◄◄ Four of the five 'Coronation' 'A4s' plus *Golden Eagle* lined up at King's Cross depot for a publicity photograph c1937. From left to right are: *Dominion of New Zealand*, *Empire of India*, *Dominion of Canada*, *Union of South Africa* (all in Garter blue) and *Golden Eagle* (in apple green). *LNER / Fox Photos / Ian Allan Library*

5

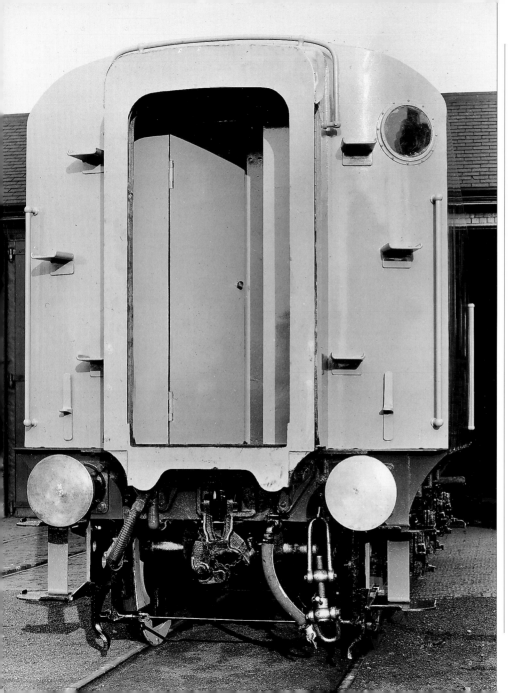

the class. Torrential rain on 12 August caused seven bridges to be swept away between Grantshouse and Reston. East Coast services were at first diverted between Newcastle, Carlisle and the Waverley Route, but on 23 August they were re-routed via Tweedmouth, Galashiels and Kelso. The overall journey between London and Edinburgh was thus extended by some 15 miles and the 'non-stop' was allowed to stop for water at Tweedmouth and for banking assistance to Falahill Summit. During late August and early September, however, nine southbound and eight northbound runs of the 'Scotsman' were made without a stop — 4082/3 miles non-stop behind steam power which (notwithstanding a USA claim dating from 1876) almost certainly remains a world record.

Until the immediate postwar years, 'A4s' were distributed among several depots, including Grantham, Doncaster and Heaton; in January 1948 there were as many as 14 at Grantham. By the autumn of 1951, however, the 19 Eastern Region 'A4s' were all at King's Cross; of the remainder, eight were based at Gateshead and seven at Haymarket. Apart from the transfer of four to Grantham for five months in 1957, this remained the position until dieselisation resulted in changes from 1962 onwards.

While the 'A4s' were clearly masters of their work, the early 1950s saw them beset by a few irritating problems which led to failures in traffic. In particular, the middle 'big end' and the right-hand driving axlebox were prone to overheating. Design modifications and changes in maintenance procedures were put in hand to cure these problems. Finally, and, not before time, the decision was taken to equip the single-chimney 'A4s' with double Kylchap chimneys. The first to be modified was No 60017 *Silver Fox* in May 1957 and the work was completed by the end of the following year. It is probably true to say that the performance of the 'A4s' in their final years equalled, if not bettered, their work before the war. Certainly the many occasions when 'A4s' were called upon to cover intensive diesel diagrams belied the fact that they represented technology which was considered out of date.

Throughout the British Railways period, one train remained the sole preserve of the 'A4s', since it required locomotives with corridor tenders. This was the new service between King's Cross and Edinburgh which replaced the non-stop summer schedule of the 'Flying Scotsman': introduced in 1949 as the 'Capitals Limited', it became the 'Elizabethan' in 1953. Contrary to popular belief, the double-chimney 'A4s' were not automatic choices for working the 'non-stop' in the years before all the 'A4s' were so equipped. In particular, *Mallard* made very infrequent appearances. Although Nos 60033 and 60034 had worked the non-stop 'Scotsman' in 1948 and 'Capitals Limited' in 1949 and 1952, it was only in the 1955 season that they shared the bulk of the King's Cross duty on the 'Elizabethan', the former also playing a major part in the following year's workings. The first choice and 'spare engine' were normally selected from those which had received a general overhaul in the spring and were nicely run-in when the 'non-stop' began in June. Haymarket had no double-chimney 'A4s' before the 1958 season (when all four of the depot's newly-equipped 'A4s' appeared on the train) so, until that year, single-chimney engines were the rule.

Between three and five 'A4s' from each of the two depots were generally employed on the 'Elizabethan' each year. The appearance of Haymarket engines was eagerly anticipated by observers in the London area, and, no doubt, Edinburgh enthusiasts were equally keen to see the King's Cross 'A4s'. The novelty did wear a little thin, however, during long runs of the Scottish engines, sometimes lasting for a month or more of the train's three-month season. The longest stint was probably that of No 60012 *Commonwealth of Australia*, which remained on the working (including the weekend trips) for 58 consecutive days in 1957. Another consistent Haymarket performer was No 60027 *Merlin*, which made more than 60 runs (40 of them consecutive) in 1959 and a record total of 76 (46 consecutive) in 1960.

Until the late 1950s, Gateshead's 'A4s' were almost as elusive in London as the Haymarket engines. There was a working every day, but it covered the up and down 'Night Scotsman' sleeper, so one had to rise early or go out late to see it. Introduction of the late-afternoon 'Talisman' service in September 1956, however, brought another of the shed's Pacifics (usually an 'A4') to London on the up train. The return leg was the following day's 10.10am from King's Cross — a train which could be observed at a more comfortable hour! A year later, through locomotive workings between King's Cross and Newcastle were reorganised and Gateshead gained more turns to London, so its 'A4s' were seen more frequently at the south end of the East Coast main line.

In spite of having on its books a number of 'A1s' and 'A3s' (the latter rejuvenated by the fitting of double chimneys from 1958 onwards), King's Cross 'Top Shed' clearly regarded its 'A4s' as its first choice for special occasions. The inaugural runs of the 'Talisman' in September 1956 and the 'Morning Talisman' in June 1957 were both worked by No 60025 *Falcon*, in September 1957 No 60015 *Quicksilver* left King's Cross with the first working of the 'Fair Maid' (an unsuccessful attempt at a Perth express), while the new 'Anglo-Scottish Car Carrier' in 1960 was entrusted to No 60032 *Gannet*.

As well as their express-passenger duties, King's Cross 'A4s' were frequently employed on stopping trains to Cambridge and Peterborough. More surprising was their almost guaranteed appearance in the late 1950s on the best-known East Coast fitted freight, the afternoon 'Scotch Goods'. This train, the 3.15pm from King's Cross freight depot to Niddrie, was referred to by many linesiders as 'the Niddrie' or, more often, by its Working Timetable reporting number, '266'. Previously worked by 'V2s', it was accelerated in the autumn of 1956 and given a fast timing to Newcastle with just one booked stop, at York, for examination. It became part of a 'top link' diagram, on which the crew returned with their Pacific from Newcastle next day on the 'Northumbrian' or, on Saturdays, the 'Flying Scotsman'. Although an 'A1' was sometimes in charge, an abiding memory of this period was the sight of an immaculate 'A4' with 40 to 50 fitted vans rattling and swaying along behind as the driver aimed to maintain the schedule as far as Tallington, where the train was booked to make its first diversion from the fast line for following expresses to pass.

On some occasions after '266' was retired to depart ahead of the 3.10 pm Newcastle express, it only reached as far as my home station of Knebworth before its first stop. There it waited on the slow line for the latter train to pass, before following it on the down fast line in order to pick up water from Langley troughs. A similar delay took place one day in April 1959 when the freight was held for the late-running 3pm to Newcastle. This was especially memorable for me as I was invited for the first time onto the footplate of an 'A4' (*Mallard*, no less!) while the train was waiting. Naturally, on this afternoon it was even more exciting than usual to watch '266' ease onto the down fast and listen to the sound reverberate from the deep cutting as the 'A4' accelerated rapidly to gain speed for the troughs, two miles distant.

A few notable events in the final years showed that the 'A4s' had lost none of their magic. On 23 May 1959,

No 60007 *Sir Nigel Gresley* worked a special train from King's Cross to Doncaster and back to mark the Golden Jubilee of the Stephenson Locomotive Society. In charge was its regular driver, Bill Hoole, a man noted — and occasionally reprimanded — for his high-speed exploits. North of Hitchin, where he had authority to run at 100mph, he accelerated 'Number Seven' to its first three-figure speed of the day. Later on the northbound run came a storming ascent of Stoke Bank, topping the summit at what may well be an all-time record of 82mph. The highlight was the return run on this stretch, when a maximum of 112mph was attained — a speed which remains a postwar speed record for steam and is today commemorated with *Mallard*-style plaques on the locomotive. That was not all, for 'the ton' was reached again on the rising gradients after passing Offord.

In spite of the increasing number of diesel locomotives, the esteem in which the 'A4s' were held was demonstrated on 8 June 1961 when the LNER Royal Train and two trains for guests ran from King's Cross to York for the wedding of HRH The Duke of Kent. The four 'A4s' (including a standby engine) prepared by 'Top Shed' were perhaps the most immaculate ever seen. That summer saw the end of steam working on the 'Elizabethan', the final down and up trains on 8 September being worked by No 60022 *Mallard* and No 60009 *Union of South Africa* respectively. There was one more opportunity for an 'A4' to run non-stop between London and Edinburgh, and this took place on 2 June 1962 when *Mallard* worked the first leg of the RCTS/SLS 'Aberdeen Flyer' railtour.

At the end of that year came the first withdrawals — five King's Cross engines, including the pioneer, *Silver Link*. Another 10 followed in 1963. All but one of them (Gateshead's No 60018) were from the Eastern Region, which was rapidly being cleared of steam traction.

When regular steam working at King's Cross ended in June 1963, the 11 'A4s' remaining at 'Top Shed' were transferred to New England. They normally worked northwards — although one often came south to Hitchin on a parcels working — but, before long, diesel non-availability and failures saw them once more bringing parcels, freight and passenger trains into London. An authorised exception to the ban on steam was made on 6 July, when *Sir Nigel Gresley* came up to work the LCGB 'Mallard Commemorative Railtour' to York and back. A repetition of the event of 25 years earlier was out of the question, but, like everyone else on board, I was secretly hoping that the 'A4' would emulate its 1959 performance on the return run. It was not quite so spectacular, but a maximum of 102mph near Essendine was immensely satisfying.

Apart from No 60008, withdrawn in July for preservation, all the New England 'A4s' appeared at King's Cross during the late summer and early autumn of 1963, making their final visits in October. Towards the end of that month, five were withdrawn and the rest transferred to Scotland. One of the former, No 60017 *Silver Fox*, actually worked up to London and took out the 6.40pm King's Cross-Leeds on 29 October — nine days after it was officially withdrawn!

At the same time, four of the remaining Gateshead 'A4s' also went to the Scottish Region, which thus found itself with no fewer than 16 of the 19 remaining 'A4s'. The new arrivals were distributed between St Margaret's and Aberdeen, but seven of them were placed in store — some at Dalry Road, where two of the original Scottish engines were even officially allocated for a short time. Within a few months, however, all were back in traffic.

Since the summer of 1962, most of the Scottish Region's 'A4s' had been based at St Rollox and Aberdeen for working Glasgow Buchanan Street-Aberdeen trains on accelerated three-hour schedules. Men at the latter depot were used to 'A4s' and other LNER Pacifics, but their colleagues at the former Caledonian and LMS shed of St Rollox regarded the new machines with some suspicion at first.

During 1964 the last three 'A4s' at Gateshead were withdrawn, along with four of the Scottish engines. Special workings, however, were to bring 'A4s' south of the border in the final years. *Union of South Africa* ran from King's Cross to Newcastle and back in October 1964, while *Kingfisher* traversed Southern Region metals on railtour duty.

Many enthusiasts from south of the border made the pilgrimage to Scotland to travel behind and photograph 'A4s' during their 'Indian summer' on the Glasgow-Aberdeen route. My own strategy was to stay at Stirling with seven-day 'Freedom of Scotland' Railrover tickets in 1965 and 1966. I could then choose to make my first journey of the day — whether travelling north or south — behind an 'A4'. The highlight of these weeks was the start of the journey on the early-evening departure from Aberdeen, with the locomotive working hard on the climb past Cove Bay in the low sunlight and amid superb coastal scenery.

I always thought that it was a fitting end to the career of the 'A4s' that they were allowed to work out their final years in fine fettle on such a demanding task. By the time of my 1966 visit, only *Bittern*, *Kingfisher* and *Lord Faringdon* were still at work — one survivor from each of the three depots which had maintained 'A4s' for most of the 1950s. With a little manipulation of a business trip to the North of England, I was able to enjoy a farewell journey behind an 'A4' on 3 September, when No 60019 *Bittern* worked a special train from Glasgow to Aberdeen and back. That was supposed to be a 'last run' for the class, but No 60024 *Kingfisher* was unexpectedly resurrected to work an Aberdeen-Glasgow service 10 days later. It returned on the 8.25am service the following morning, 14 September 1966 — 31 years to the day since *Silver Link* made its first revenue-earning trip.

So the career of the 'A4s' came to an end. Six have been preserved, and for those of us who saw them in day-to-day service it is sobering to think that they have survived for an even longer time in the preservation era and that many people have only seen them in this period. At a station on a heritage railway a few years ago, I noticed someone gazing at *Sir Nigel Gresley* for a good 10 minutes, totally oblivious to everything else that was going on. This was no impressionable youngster seeing an 'A4' for the first time, but a hard-nosed journalist from a national railway magazine! Say what you like about any other class of steam locomotive; the 'A4' is the only one which is awe-inspiring enough — even when stationary — to command such rapturous attention.

David Percival
October 2000

When only three months old, on 30 June 1938, No 4469 *Gadwall* passes Brookman Park at the head of the up 'Silver Jubilee', although the train appears to consist of blue streamlined stock. The locomotive was destroyed in an air raid in York on 29 April 1942, when the shed was hit by a bomb. It was allocated to Gateshead throughout its brief career of just over four years, and was attached to a non-corridor tender, as were the other Gateshead 'A4s'.
E. R. Wethersett / Ian Allan Library

LNER No 4469

Built	March 1938 (Works No 1871)
Names	Originally *Gadwall*; renamed *Sir Ralph Wedgwood* March 1939.
Liveries	Originally LNER Garter blue
	Black April 1942
Allocations	Gateshead from new
Withdrawn	June 1942 after being bombed in York shed 29 April 1942.

BR No 60001 (LNER No 4500)

Built	Doncaster April 1938 (Works No 1873)
Names	Originally *Garganey*; renamed *Sir Ronald Matthews* March 1939
Numbers	LNER No 4500 from new
	LNER No 1, November 1946 (No 609 allocated but not carried)
	BR No 60001 July 1948
Double chimney fitted	April 1958
Liveries	Originally LNER Garter blue
	Black December 1941
	LNER Garter blue November 1946
	BR blue February 1950
	BR green August 1951
Allocations	Gateshead from new until withdrawal
Withdrawn	October 1964; cut up at Hughes of Blyth

▼ Only days before the streamlined trains were withdrawn due to the outbreak of war, No 4500 *Sir Ronald Matthews* passes Sandy at the head of the up 'Flying Scotsman' on 28 August 1939. The locomotive was the only member of the class to remain at the same depot (Gateshead) during its entire working career, with the exception of No 4469 *Gadwall*, withdrawn after only four years' service. *E. R. Wethersett /*
Ian Allan Library

▲ Looking extremely clean for a Gateshead Pacific, No 60001 *Sir Ronald Matthews* leaves Newcastle across the River Tyne at the head of the up 'Flying Scotsman' in the early 1950s. The regular 'A4' on this diagram at this period was No 60016 *Silver King*, the locomotive working as far as Grantham. No 60001 was the first to receive BR lined green livery, in August 1951. *Eric Treacy*

11

No 4499 was still carrying the name *Pochard* when it was photographed leaving King's Cross on a down express on 8 January 1939. This locomotive was the first to have the cut-off increased from 65 to 75% in March 1943, this modification subsequently being applied to the rest of the class. This alteration had been necessary due to the very heavy trains the class were required to haul during the war years. *Ian Allan Library*

BR No 60002 (LNER No 4499)

Built	Doncaster April 1938 (Works No 1872)
Names	Originally *Pochard*; renamed *Sir Murrough Wilson* April 1939
Numbers	LNER No 4499 from new
	LNER No 2, October 1946 (No 608 allocated but not carried)
	BR No 60002 May 1948
Double chimney fitted	July 1957
Liveries	Originally LNER Garter blue
	Black February 1942
	LNER Garter blue November 1946
	BR blue February 1950
	BR green August 1951
Allocations	Gateshead from new
	King's Cross August 1943
	Gateshead October 1943
Withdrawn	May 1964; scrapped George Cohen at Cargo Fleet

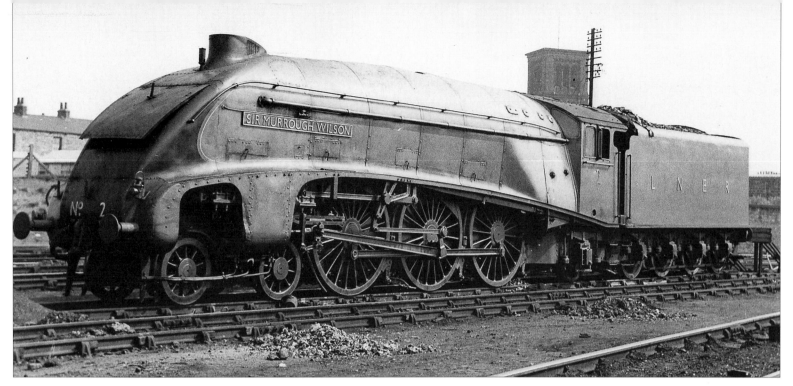

This picture is undated, but must have been between October 1946 and May 1948 as it is carrying No 2 and the Garter blue livery. *Ian Allan Library*

This was probably No 60002's last visit to King's Cross shed, as the picture is dated July 1963 — one month after 'Top Shed' closed. No doubt the locomotive had worked up to King's Cross due to a diesel failure. Looking very clean for an 'A4' during this period, it cannot have had long to go before being stored at Heaton shed, although still officially allocated to Gateshead. Apart from a brief spell at King's Cross in 1943, it was a Gateshead locomotive throughout its working life and, like many of the Tyneside 'A4s', was seldom in the limelight. *G. H. Wheeler*

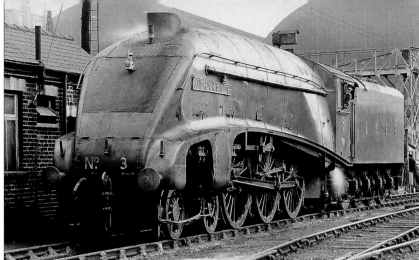

No 4494 *Andrew K. McCosh* presents a sorry sight in its dirty black livery with 'NE' on its tender as it heads a King's Cross-Leeds train past New Southgate on 20 July 1946.
E. R. Wethersett / Ian Allan Library

No 3 had been restored to its fine blue livery during a works visit to Doncaster in June 1947. It is seen between duties in the locomotive yard at King's Cross, having worked a local train, judging by the position of the lamp. The picture is undated, but was taken between June 1947, when the locomotive had its middle cylinder reduced to 17in diameter, and July 1949, when it was renumbered 60003. The cylinder reverted to normal (18½in) June 1954. *Ian Allan Library*

BR No 60003 (LNER No 4494)

Built	Doncaster August 1937 (Works No 1859)
Names	Originally *Osprey*; renamed *Andrew K. McCosh* October 1942
Numbers	LNER No 4494 from new
	LNER No 3, September 1946 (No 596 allocated but not carried)
	BR No 60003 July 1949
Double chimney fitted	July 1957
Liveries	Originally LNER apple green
	LNER Garter blue October 1938
	Black August 1942
	LNER Garter blue June 1947
	BR blue April 1950
	BR green October 1951
Allocations	Heaton from new
	Doncaster January 1938
	Grantham April 1938
	Doncaster March 1939
	King's Cross May 1939
	Grantham January 1941
	King's Cross February 1941
	Grantham April 1957
	King's Cross September 1957
Withdrawn	December 1962; cut up Doncaster Works

This superb picture shows the locomotive in fine postwar King's Cross condition at the head of the down 'Yorkshire Pullman' near Woolmer Green on 16 May 1952. During that month the locomotive was used on trials between King's Cross and Doncaster with different loads, to see if schedules could be cut. It was selected to haul one of the Royal specials from King's Cross to York on 8 June 1961 in connection with the wedding of HRH The Duke of Kent. *E. R. Wethersett / Ian Allan Library*

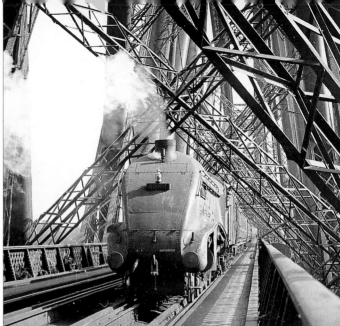

A fine study of No 4462 *Great Snipe* when only about a year old, heading a down express past New Southgate in 1938. It was the first of the class during a works visit in June 1941 to have the skirting removed, but only behind the cylinders, although two other members of the class had this completely removed in July 1941. *E. R. Wethersett / Ian Allan Library*

Not in the external condition normally associated with Haymarket shed, No 60004 *William Whitelaw* heads a local service across the Forth Bridge. The picture is undated, but was probably taken in the early 1950s. *E. R. Wethersett / Ian Allan Library*

BR No 60004 (LNER No 4462)

Built	Doncaster November 1937 (Works No 1864)
Names	Originally *Great Snipe*; renamed *William Whitelaw* July 1941
Numbers	Originally LNER No 4462
	LNER No 4, August 1946 (No 601 allocated but not carried)
	BR No 60004 May 1948
Double chimney fitted	December 1957
Liveries	Originally LNER Garter blue
	Black October 1942
	LNER Garter blue November 1946
	BR blue August 1950
	BR green February 1952
Allocations	King's Cross from new
	Gateshead February 1938
	Heaton June 1940
	Haymarket July 1941
	Aberdeen June 1962
	Haymarket September 1962
	Aberdeen June 1963
Withdrawn	July 1966; cut up Motherwell Machinery & Scrap Co at Wishaw

The locomotive hauled several railtours. On 2 March 1962 it took over the 'Aberdeen Flyer' from King's Cross to Aberdeen at Edinburgh for the journey north, and on 30 June 1963 headed the Railway Correspondence & Travel Society's 'Three Summits Tour' at Auchinleck for the journey to Carlisle, giving a very poor performance. On 19 September 1965 it hauled the RCTS 'Blyth-Tyne Tour' from Leeds to Eaglescliffe and thence to Newcastle via Bishop Auckland, where it is shown passing underneath the impressive signal gantry. *Gavin Morrison*

This is an official but undated photograph, but was probably taken in September 1942 when the locomotive received the wartime black livery and was renamed *Charles H. Newton* as shown. (It was originally *Capercaillie* when it entered service in June 1938.) After June 1943, the name was altered again to *Sir Charles Newton*, which it retained until withdrawal.

This locomotive was the only one of the four originally fitted with Kylchap blastpipes that was not allocated to King's Cross shed, and never seemed to be in the limelight during its career, as were Nos 4468, 4902 and 4903 (BR Nos 60022, 60033 and 60034). Like the other Gateshead-allocated 'A4s', it seems to have been photographed infrequently, by comparison to the King's Cross and Haymarket locomotives, and, apart from short spells at St Margaret's and Ferryhill before withdrawal, it was never allocated to anywhere other than Gateshead. It became the last of the class to have its maximum cut-off increased to 75% in forward gear, this being done in 1957. No 4901 was one of 12 which received just the 'NE' on the tender; until July 1942, those which were painted black had received 'LNER'. It was the last of the class to lose its metal cabside number and letters on the tender, in January 1948. *Ian Allan Library*

BR No 60005 (LNER No 4901)

Built	Doncaster June 1938 (Works No 1875)
Names	Originally *Capercaillie*; renamed *Charles H. Newton* September 1942
	and again as *Sir Charles Newton* June 1943
Numbers	Originally LNER No 4901
	LNER No 5, August 1946 (No 611 allocated but not carried)
	BR No 60005 July 1948
Double chimney fitted	From new
Liveries	Originally LNER Garter blue
	Black October 1942
	LNER Garter blue August 1946
	BR blue November 1949
	BR green November 1952
Allocations	Gateshead from new
	St Margaret's October 1963
	Aberdeen November 1963
Withdrawn	March 1964; cut up George H. Campbell at Airdrie

Now No 60005, *Sir Charles Newton* is working hard up the 1 in 190 gradient near the 'Borders' sign between Berwick and Burnmouth on a down train of fish vans on 25 July 1952. The King's Cross 'A4s' were regularly diagrammed to work express-goods trains in the postwar years. The locomotive's external condition was typical for most of the Gateshead Pacifics around this period.

In April 1940 this locomotive was recorded as covering the 25 miles between Otterington and Poppleton Junction in 19min 57sec, averaging 75.9mph with a 22-coach train — 730 tons gross! *E. R. Wethersett / Ian Allan Library*

No 4466 *Herring Gull* was one of the 14 'A4s' ordered in November 1936 which were all turned out in Garter blue with streamlined non-corridor tenders and painted numbers. It is pictured at Newcastle Central at the head of an up express during 1938, its first year in service. *R. E. Kirkbright*

Now in the postwar LNER Garter blue which it had received two months prior to this photograph being taken on 7 June 1947, No 4466 *Herring Gull* has now become No 6, and has been renamed *Sir Ralph Wedgwood*, the name change occurring in January 1944. The lamps indicate the train is an express, although the rolling stock visible out of Copenhagen Tunnel hardly gives that impression. *E. R. Wethersett / Ian Allan Library*

BR No 60006 (LNER Nos 4446, 605)

Built	Doncaster January 1938 (Works No 1868)
Names	Originally *Herring Gull*; renamed *Sir Ralph Wedgwood* January 1944
Numbers	Originally LNER No 4466
	LNER No 605 January 1946
	LNER No 6, May 1946
	BR No 60006 December 1948
Double chimney fitted	April 1958
Liveries	Originally LNER Garter blue
	Black April 1942
	LNER Garter blue April 1947
	BR blue March 1950
	BR green August 1952
Allocations	King's Cross from new
	Grantham April 1938
	King's Cross August 1944
	New England June 1963
	St Margaret's October 1963
	Aberdeen May 1964
Withdrawn	September 1965; cut up Motherwell Machinery & Scrap Co at Wishaw

No 4498 was the last of the second batch of 'A4s' ordered, of which there were 17. It happened to be the 100th Pacific built by Nigel Gresley, and as a tribute to him it was named *Sir Nigel Gresley*. This fine undated picture must have been taken after February 1938, as it only received the gold with red shielded numbers after this date. The embossed steel numbers and letters were fitted during its first general overhaul.

Due to its name, this was always a high-profile locomotive, and no doubt the famous prewar Hornby 'OO' model also increased its popularity. However, records show it was not one of the locomotives to attain incredible feats of continuous days running on the 'Coronation' and 'West Riding' streamlined trains — in fact it was never officially allocated to these turns, although no doubt it did appear on occasions. It was not until many years later — in the 1950s, when it was allocated to the famous driver, Bill Hoole — that it began to be noticed for some outstanding performances. Here it is shown heading a heavy down express, believed to be near Ganwick. *E. R. Wethersett*

BR No 60007 (LNER No 4498)

Built	Doncaster November 1937 (Works No 1863)
Name	*Sir Nigel Gresley*
Numbers	Originally LNER No 4498
	LNER No 7, January 1947 (No 600 allocated but not carried)
	BR No 60007 March 1948
Double chimney fitted	December 1957
Liveries	Originally LNER Garter blue
	Black February 1942
	LNER Garter blue March 1947
	BR blue September 1950
	BR green April 1952
Allocations	King's Cross from new
	Grantham April 1944
	King's Cross June 1950
	New England June 1963
	St Margaret's October 1963
	Aberdeen July 1964
Withdrawn	February 1966; to Crewe Works for overhaul July 1966; preserved by the A4 Locomotive Society

In the 1950s and early 1960s No 60007 continued to be allocated to King's Cross. While it does not seem to have been employed on the non-stop services to Edinburgh, it was one of the top-link engines and was eventually allocated to driver Bill Hoole as 'his' engine.

Here it is seen in immaculate condition climbing Holloway Bank at the head of the 'Stephenson Jubilee' organised by the Stephenson Locomotive Society from King's Cross to Doncaster on 23 May 1959. It was driven by Bill Hoole, who gave the lucky passengers a day out they will never forget. The magic 100mph was reached and exceeded three times, and the climb up Stoke Bank was a record as the train was doing 82mph as it reached the summit. On the return, 112mph was recorded down Stoke, giving an average of 99.5mph from the summit to Tallington, and to cap it all 100mph

was attained at Sandy, which was unheard of at this location on the up line. The authorities must have wondered if progress was really being made with the introduction of the Class 40s — these figures would have done credit to a 'Deltic'. Following this event No 60007 became a star locomotive and, after steam finished at King's Cross, enjoyed a brief spell on the Glasgow-Aberdeen services, before entering preservation.

Since its return to steam on the main lines in 1972, *Sir Nigel Gresley* has been working specials all over the network, as well as visiting many preserved lines, and is thus probably almost as well known as *Mallard* and *Flying Scotsman*.
E. R. Wethersett

A fine official photograph shows No 4496 *Golden Shuttle* as it appeared when new. It was first allocated to Doncaster, but stayed for less than one month, spending the rest of its career shared between King's Cross and Grantham, except for its final month before withdrawal. Along with No 4495 *Golden Fleece* it was allocated to the streamlined 'West Riding' train which began operating on 27 September 1935. In fact during a period in 1939 it worked for 15 weeks consecutively, with only two days off; in total, it worked 277 of the 968 'West Riding' trains run. It ran with a corridor tender until April 1957 when it received a non-corridor. *Ian Allan Library*

In September 1945 No 4496 was renamed *Dwight D. Eisenhower* in honour of the Supreme Commander, Allied Forces (Europe), during World War 2. In this photograph, taken following its 1946 renumbering as No 8, it is working a Newcastle-King's Cross express. The locomotive carries LNER Garter blue, and was the first 'A4' restored to this livery after the war, on the occasion of its renaming.

Latterly BR No 60008, *Dwight D. Eisenhower* was withdrawn in July 1963. In view of its US associations, at a ceremony on 27 April 1964 this locomotive was handed over by Dr Beeching to the National Railway Museum of Green Bay, Wisconsin, where it has remained as a static exhibit to this day. *R. F. Dearden*

Built	Doncaster September 1937 (Works No 1861)
Names	Originally *Golden Shuttle*; renamed *Dwight D. Eisenhower* September 1945
Numbers	Originally LNER No 4496
	LNER No 8, November 1946 (No 598 allocated but not carried)
	BR No 60008 October 1948
Double chimney fitted	August 1958
Liveries	Originally LNER Garter blue
	Black January 1942
	LNER Garter blue September 1945
	BR blue June 1950
	BR green November 1951
Allocations	Doncaster from new
	King's Cross September 1937
	Grantham December 1939
	King's Cross June 1950
	Grantham April 1957
	King's Cross September 1957
	New England June 1963
Withdrawn	July 1963; preserved at the National Railway Museum of Green Bay, Wisconsin, USA

BR No 60009 (LNER No 4488)

Built	Doncaster September 1937 (Works No 1853)
Name	*Union of South Africa*.
Numbers	Originally LNER No 4488
	LNER No 9, January 1947 (No 590 allocated but not carried)
	BR No 60009 May 1948
Double chimney fitted	November 1958
Liveries	Originally LNER Garter blue
	Black March 1942
	LNER Garter blue February 1947
	BR blue August 1949
	BR green October 1952
Allocations	Haymarket from new
	Aberdeen May 1962
Withdrawn	June 1966; preserved

▲ Even before preservation, *Union of South Africa* was probably the most famous of the Haymarket 'A4s'. When new it was one of the five selected for the arduous 'Coronation' streamline express, which train consisted of eight coaches plus a 'beaver-tail' observation car. In this picture of the locomotive and train heading north the hand-painted coat of arms of the 'Union' can just be discerned under the cabside number.

The locomotive achieved the highest mileage between repairs for a Class A4, running 126,814 miles between November 1950 and August 1952; it also achieved the highest mileage for the class, with around 1,900,000 in LNER and BR service. Other notable events during its career were the haulage of the first postwar non-stop up 'Flying Scotsman' (in June 1948), the first up 'Elizabethan' (in June 1953), and the last up 'Elizabethan' (in September 1961). *Ian Allan Library*

◄ No 60009 *Union of South Africa* was the last 'A4' to receive a general repair, this being carried out at Doncaster in November 1963, just before 'The Plant' finished steam overhauls. It had the sad duty of working the last 'A4'-hauled train out of King's Cross — the RCTS/SLS 'Jubilee Requiem' — on 24 October 1964. The picture shows the special ready to leave Newcastle Central on the return working, when it achieved 96mph down Stoke Bank and arrived back no less than 26min early.

Prior to its withdrawal, the locomotive put in nearly three years' service on Aberdeen-Glasgow expresses. In June 1966, after a period in store at Ferryhill, it was moved to Thornton depot, where it was reinstated to work the last steam-hauled special in the Scottish Region — a massive train of 18 coaches, weighing 640 tons — which it shared for part of the journey with Stanier Class 5 No 44997. No 60009 then passed into preservation, owned by Mr John Cameron. *Gavin Morrison*

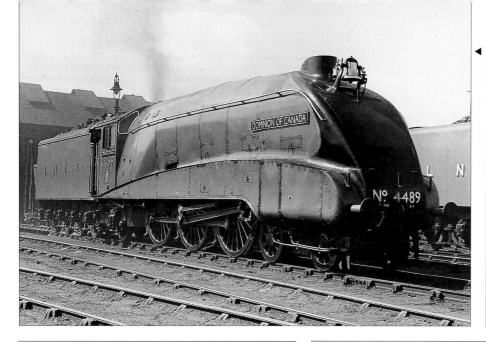

A superb portrait of *Dominion of Canada* at 'Top Shed', King's Cross, on 22 April 1939. The bell presented by the Canadian Pacific Railway Co was fitted in March 1938, and it remained with the locomotive until the double chimney was added in December 1957. The CPR also presented the locomotive with a special five-note chrome whistle on 15 June 1937; this was removed in April 1949 and bought by the Festiniog Railway, but regrettably was stolen during Christmas 1967. Canada's coat of arms can be seen on the side of the cab.

No 4489 was originally allocated the name *Buzzard*, but received *Woodcock* instead. The locomotive ran in 'shop' grey livery between 4 and 17 May 1937, before returning to Doncaster Works in June to receive Garter blue livery, as it was one of the five locomotives allocated to the 'Coronation' streamlined express service, which commenced on 3 July 1937. Before leaving the works it was renamed *Dominion of Canada*. It hauled the press trip for the 'Coronation' on 30 June 1937 from King's Cross to Barkston, attaining 109.5mph down Stoke Bank on the return, in the hands of driver G. Burfoot of King's Cross.

During the summer of 1939 *Dominion of Canada* covered 18,327 miles in seven weeks, which involved two weeks on the 'Coronation', four weeks on the 'Flying Scotsman' and one on the 'West Riding'. *E. R. Wethersett / Ian Allan Library*

By the date of this photograph — 29 July 1950 — *Dominion of Canada* had lost its metal numbers and was numbered 60010 with 'BRITISH RAILWAYS' on the tender, although it was still in Garter blue livery. The picture shows it storming north past New Southgate on a Newcastle express. Apart from a five-month break at Grantham in 1957, it remained at King's Cross until Top Shed closed in June 1963, after which it had a short spell at Aberdeen Ferryhill. *E. R. Wethersett*

BR No 60010 (LNER No 4489)

Built	Doncaster May 1937 (Works No 1854)
Names	Originally *Woodcock*; renamed *Dominion of Canada* June 1937
Numbers	Originally LNER No 4489
	LNER No 10, May 1946 (No 591 allocated but not carried)
	BR No 60010 October 1948
Double chimney fitted	December 1957
Liveries	Originally LNER Garter blue*
	Black February 1942
	LNER Garter blue November 1947
	BR blue September 1950
	BR green May 1952
	* Note: The locomotive entered service in works grey with green-painted wheels
Allocations	King's Cross from new
	Grantham April 1957
	King's Cross September 1957
	New England June 1963
	Aberdeen October 1963
Withdrawn	May 1965 preserved at the Canadian Railroad Historical Association, near Montreal

In May 1965 the Scottish Region sent No 60010 to Darlington Works for repair, but due to the state of its boiler the locomotive was condemned instead. It languished at Darlington until it was towed to Crewe Works on 27 April 1966 by 'Standard 4MT' No 75019; this picture shows the ensemble leaving Neville Hill yard at Leeds. The 'A4' was returned to good external condition at a cost of £1,600, before being presented by the BRB to the acting High Commissioner for Canada, at a ceremony aboard the MV *Beaveroak* at the Royal Victoria Dock in London. It has since been displayed in Montreal at the Canadian Railroad Historical Museum.
Gavin Morrison

Empire of India spent 24 years allocated to Haymarket. However, it went new to King's Cross, where it spent nine months before moving north of the border; this picture was taken during that period on 17 July 1937 alongside 'A3' No 4480 *Enterprise*. The 'A4' was a regular performer on the 'Coronation', and is recorded as having hauled the train on 100 occasions. The locomotive's hand-painted coat of arms is clearly visible on the cabside. *E. R. Wethersett / Ian Allan Library*

Humble work for No 60011 as it heads a six-coach Edinburgh to Aberdeen local across the Forth Bridge, which it would have taken over at Dundee. The bridge workers appear more interested in the photographer than the immaculate locomotive passing them.

The locomotive received its last overhaul at Doncaster during May 1962, and upon its return to Scotland was transferred to Aberdeen Ferryhill, where it did nearly two years' work on Aberdeen-Glasgow expresses. It was one of two 'A4s' to visit Inverurie Works for attention, in October 1962, the other being No 60004, two months earlier. *E. R. Wethersett / Ian Allan Library*

BR No 60011 (LNER No 4490)

Built	Doncaster June 1937 (Works No 1855)
Name	*Empire of India*
Numbers	Originally LNER No 4490
	LNER No 11, November 1946 (No 592 allocated but not carried)
	BR No 60011 March 1949
Double chimney fitted	January 1958
Liveries	Originally LNER Garter blue
	Black October 1942
	LNER Garter blue November 1946
	BR blue June 1950
	BR green April 1952
Allocations	King's Cross from new
	Haymarket March 1938
	Aberdeen June 1962
Withdrawn	May 1964; cut up Darlington Works

BR No 60012 (LNER No 4491)

Built	Doncaster June 1937 (Works No 1856)
Name	*Commonwealth of Australia*
Numbers	Originally LNER No 4491
	LNER No 12, January 1947 (No 593 allocated but not carried)
	BR No 60012 May 1948
Double chimney fitted	July 1958
Liveries	Originally LNER Garter blue
	Black September 1942
	LNER Garter blue August 1947
	BR blue August 1949
	BR green November 1952
Allocations	Haymarket from new (Polmadie on loan 1949)
	Dalry Road September 1963
	Aberdeen January 1964
Withdrawn	August 1964; cut up Motherwell Machinery & Scrap Co, Wishaw

▼ The begrimed crew on ex-Great Northern Class N1 No 4578 admire the immaculate No 4491 and 'West Riding' coaches as they enter King's Cross, no doubt on time. King's Cross must have borrowed the locomotive from its normal 'Coronation' duties, as Nos 4495 and 4496 were the regular locomotives on this train. The picture dates from c1938.
H. Gordon Tidey /Ian Allan Library

▲ *Commonwealth of Australia* was one of the five 'A4s' to be assigned from new to the 'Coronation'; it went to Haymarket, where it spent virtually all its working days. It was selected to haul the inaugural down 'Coronation' on 3 July 1937, reaching York in 2hr 35min 36sec, in the capable hands of driver T. Dron of Gateshead. It hauled 48 of the first 51 'Coronation' trains, covering 23,000 miles including the balancing workings. The picture shows it during this achievement, climbing Cockburnspath in August 1937. *E. R. Wethersett / Ian Allan Library*

▲

In spotless condition No 60012 *Commonwealth of Australia* coasts past the shed yard at York at the head of the non-stop Edinburgh Waverley-King's Cross 'Elizabethan' on 14 September 1957. It was one of two locomotives to retain the 17in middle cylinder reduction modification to the end of its career (the other being No 60020 *Guillemot* of Gateshead). During 1949 it was loaned to Polmadie shed in Glasgow for working the West Coast main line to Carlisle; during the 1950s Haymarket's Class A1s were similarly sent on loan during the summer months. In 1960 No 60012 had its chime whistle replaced by a multi-note one, which was presented by Capt Howey, owner of the Romney, Hythe & Dymchurch Railway, who had obtained it from a Western Australian locomotive. *Gavin Morrison*

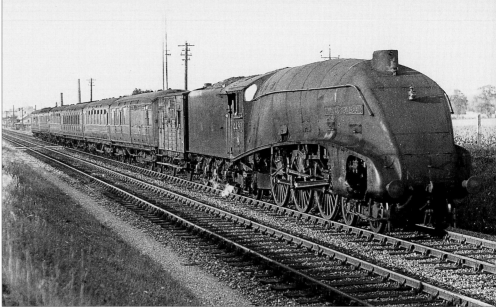

BR No 60013 (LNER No 4492)

Built	Doncaster June 1937 (Works No 1857)
Name	*Dominion of New Zealand*
Numbers	Originally LNER No 4492
	LNER No 13, August 1946 (No 594 allocated but not carried)
	BR No 60013 May 1949
Double chimney fitted	July 1958
Liveries	Originally LNER Garter blue
	Black November 1941
	LNER Garter blue August 1946
	BR blue May 1949
	BR green October 1952
Allocations	King's Cross from new
	Haymarket July 1937
	King's Cross March 1938
	Grantham May 1948
	King's Cross June 1950
Withdrawn	April 1963; cut up Doncaster Works

▼ There seems to be a crowd at the end of the platform to see No 4492 *Dominion of New Zealand* depart Edinburgh Waverley with the up 'Flying Scotsman' on 20 August 1937. During this period the locomotive worked no fewer than 62 turns between King's Cross and Edinburgh, 52 of them consecutively. Note the amount of coal in the tender, which appears to be well above the cab roof.

The locomotive ran with a corridor tender until 1950, and then had a five-year period attached to a streamlined non-corridor, before receiving another corridor tender. It had a standard chrome whistle for two years, but in May 1939 was fitted with a New Zealand Government Railways whistle which had a lower tone than the others. When withdrawn this whistle was bought by the Festiniog Railway, but, like the one from No 4489, this also got stolen. *E. R. Wethersett / Ian Allan Library*

▲ The shabby condition of No 4492 shown here is in sharp contrast to the earlier picture. The locomotive carries wartime black, with only 'NE' on the tender, although the metal numbers are still on the cabside. It is seen passing Shepreth working a humble Cambridge-King's Cross stopping train on 13 July 1945. *E. R. Wethersett / Ian Allan Library*

This superb picture taken at Potters Bar shows the 'Silver Jubilee' express travelling at 75mph on its record-breaking trial run, which was to change the face of East Coast main line travel until the outbreak of war. It took place on 27 September 1935 from King's Cross to Grantham, only three days before the train entered service. The performance was outstanding, with 112mph being recorded twice and 70 miles covered at an average speed of 91.8mph; the train was driven by driver A. Taylor with fireman J. Luty. Even more remarkable was the fact that the locomotive was built in three months between 26 June and September 1935. It then worked the 'Silver Jubilee' for the first three weeks, covering 8,000 miles without failure until the second locomotive, *Quicksilver*, was ready for service.

The livery was totally new: the smokebox casing was painted dark charcoal grey, side skirtings and frames were battleship grey, and the remainder was silver-grey without any lining. As can be seen in the photograph, the locomotive name was painted on the boiler casing. After about nine months, the locomotive number was applied to the front in shaded numerals.

Somebody on the train is giving a friendly wave to the people who had turned out to witness the memorable occasion.
E. R. Wethersett / Ian Allan Library

▲ **BR No 60014 (LNER No 2509)**

Built	Doncaster September 1935 (Works No 1818)
Name	*Silver Link*
Numbers	Originally LNER No 2509
	LNER No 14, June 1946 (No 580 allocated but not carried)
	BR No 60014 June 1949
Double chimney fitted	October 1957
Liveries	Originally grey
	LNER Garter blue December 1937
	Black December 1941
	LNER Garter blue June 1946
	BR blue June 1949
	BR green January 1952
Allocations	King's Cross from new
	Grantham August 1944
	King's Cross May 1948
	Grantham June 1948
	King's Cross May 1950
Withdrawn	December 1962; cut up Doncaster Works

In December 1937 *Silver Link* received LNER Garter blue livery, which had been adopted as standard for the class. The locomotive also received brass nameplates which were chromium-painted; those on Nos 2509 and 2510 had rounded corners, whereas the plates on the remainder of the class had squared corners.

On 5 April 1940 this locomotive was recorded as hauling the 1pm from King's Cross with Driver Carme of Grantham at the controls, when it took a 25-coach train of 850 tons north, needing 16min to pass Finsbury Park but then covering the 103 miles to Grantham in 2hr 3min! *Ian Allan Library*

In June 1946 *Silver Link* was renumbered 14, and is seen here with this number at Ganwick at the head of an Edinburgh-King's Cross express on 18 April 1949. It did not receive its BR number (60014) until June 1949. Note that the cast letter 'R' is missing from the tender. *E. R. Wethersett / Ian Allan Library*

Silver Link in later life, as No 60014 in BR green livery, at the head of the up 'Norseman' near Stevenage on 1 August 1955.

Unfortunately *Silver Link* was one of the first of the class to be withdrawn, and languished at Doncaster Works hoping that somebody would buy it; sadly this was not to be. Surely, of all the 'A4s', this one should have been preserved. It worked 564 of the 1,509 'Silver Jubilee' trains run, and had 32 outings on the 'Coronation' and 12 on the 'West Riding'. Of the 4,004 streamlined trains operated it worked 608 — what an achievement. It will always be associated in the 1950s and early 1960s with the famous King's Cross driver, Ted Hailstone, who kept the locomotive in immaculate condition, and who could always be relied upon to give a sparkling performance. In 1953 it hauled one of the 'Plant' (Doncaster Works) centenary specials, and on 8 June 1961 worked one of the Royal specials for HRH The Duke of Kent's wedding, having had its cab roof painted white for the occasion. *E. R. Wethersett / Ian Allan Library*

A high proportion of the pictures published over the years of the 'Silver Jubilee' were taken south of Peterborough. Here we see it much further north heading south from Chaloner's Whin Junction near York, on the now-abandoned section of the East Coast main line. By the date of this photograph, 16 August 1937, the locomotive had received its front number. *Quicksilver* entered service two weeks after *Silver Link*, and became the first 'A4' to visit Edinburgh on 19 November 1935. It is recorded as having worked the 'Silver Jubilee' 456 times out of the total of 1,509. Apart from its brief allocation to Gateshead in 1936, it remained a King's Cross and Grantham locomotive until withdrawal. *E. R. Wethersett / Ian Allan Library*

BR No 60015 (LNER No 2510)

Built	Doncaster September 1935 (Works No 1819)		
Name	*Quicksilver*		
Numbers	Originally LNER No 2510		
	LNER No 15, September 1946 (No 581 allocated but not carried)		
	BR No 60015 December 1948		
Double chimney fitted	August 1957	**Allocations**	King's Cross from new
Liveries	Originally grey		Gateshead December 1936
	LNER Garter blue May 1938		King's Cross January 1937
	Black October 1943		Grantham August 1944
	LNER Garter blue October 1947		King's Cross September 1951
	BR blue November 1949	**Withdrawn**	April 1963;
	BR green November 1951		cut up Doncaster Works

After a week or two at King's Cross, *Silver King* was sent to Gateshead to act as the standby locomotive for the up 'Silver Jubilee'. It then remained on Tyneside until going to Scotland for its last 18 months in traffic. It led a less high-profile existence than the other three King's Cross 'Silver Jubilee' locomotives. In fact, due to the high reliability of Nos 2509, 2510 and 2512, it only worked the train on 80 occasions out of the 1,509 times it ran. *Silver King* settled down to a regular diagram working a down train to Edinburgh after the 'Silver Jubilee' had departed at 10.00am. It then headed south on a working to Leeds and returned during the night to Gateshead, so, although Haymarket did not receive its first 'A4s' until the end of 1936, No 2511 was almost a daily visitor since October 1935. Here it is shown in original condition. *W. J. Reynolds*

Silver King heading the up 'Postal' in the Glen of Caron Water in July 1964. *E. Oldham*

BR No 60016 (LNER No 2511)

Built	Doncaster November 1935 (Works No 1818)		
Name	*Silver King*		
Numbers	Originally LNER No 2511	**Allocations**	King's Cross from new
	LNER No 16, November 1946		Gateshead November 1935
	(No 582 allocated but not carried)		Heaton November 1939
	BR No 60016 June 1948		Gateshead March 1943
Double chimney fitted	June 1957		Heaton May 1943
Liveries	Originally grey		Gateshead January 1945
	LNER Garter blue August 1938		St Margaret's October 1963
	Black April 1943		Aberdeen November 1963
	LNER Garter blue May 1947	**Withdrawn**	March 1965; cut up Motherwell
	BR blue October 1949		Machinery & Scrap Co at
	BR green July 1952		Wishaw

▼ *Silver King* was the only one of the four 'Silver Jubilee' locomotives to run attached to a non-corridor tender, which it received in June 1948, and which it then retained. In the early 1950s it was a regular performer on the up 'Flying Scotsman' from Newcastle to Grantham, returning north on the 3pm from King's Cross.

The locomotive was transferred to Scotland in October 1963, initially to St Margaret's and then Aberdeen Ferryhill for 18 months before withdrawal. It is shown on the 5.30pm Glasgow to Aberdeen near Gleneagles in April 1964. *W. J. V. Anderson*

BR No 60017 (LNER No 2512)

Built	Doncaster December 1935
	(Works No 1823)
Name	*Silver Fox*
Numbers	Originally LNER No 2512
	LNER No 17, September 1946
	(No 583 allocated but not carried)
	BR No 60017 June 1949
Double chimney fitted	May 1957
Liveries	Originally grey
	LNER Garter blue
	November 1937
	Black November 1941
	LNER Garter blue
	September 1947
	BR blue September 1950
	BR green December 1951
Allocations	King's Cross from new
	New England June 1963
Withdrawn	October 1963; cut up
	Doncaster Works

Silver Fox was the last of the 'Silver Jubilee' locomotives to enter service, in December 1935 at King's Cross shed. It remained at 'Top Shed' until three months before withdrawal. It is recorded as having hauled the train on 409 out of the possible 1,509 occasions. As can be seen in both pictures it carried a stainless steel fox on both sides of the boiler casing. These were presented by Samuel Fox & Co Ltd, Steel Manufacturers, and both were retained until its end. This photograph shows it at the head of the up 'Silver Jubilee' near Marshmoor on 9 June 1937. *E. R. Wethersett / Ian Allan Library*

This portrait shows the locomotive in immaculate external condition waiting to take over an up express just outside Doncaster station on 29 April 1962. It was the first of the class to receive the Kylchap double blastpipe and chimney, in May 1957, apart from the four locomotives (Nos 4468, 4901, 4902 and 4903) which were so fitted from new. It also had the sad duty of working the last regular 'A4' working out of King's Cross on 29 October 1963, this being the 18.40 to Leeds. *Gavin Morrison*

BR No 60018 (LNER No 4463)

Built	Doncaster December 1937 (Works No 1864)
Name	*Sparrow Hawk*
Numbers	Originally LNER No 4463
	LNER No 18, September 1946 (No 602 allocated but not carried)
	BR No 60018 October 1948
Double chimney fitted	October 1957
Liveries	Originally LNER Garter blue
	Black August 1943
	LNER Garter blue December 1946
	BR blue April 1950
	BR green October 1951
Allocations	Gateshead from new
	Heaton October 1940
	Gateshead March 1943
	Heaton May 1943
	Gateshead November 1945
Withdrawn	June 1963; cut up Doncaster Works

▼ If one examines carefully the many books that have been produced on the Class A4s, one notices that *Sparrow Hawk* is conspicuous by its absence in the photographs, especially in the postwar years. This fine photograph shows it in original condition at the head of a down express near Hadley Wood. *Ian Allan Library*

▲ As BR No 60018, *Sparrow Hawk* drifts down from Stoke Summit towards Grantham on a northbound goods; this was a running-in turn following a general repair — most likely the locomotive's last before being fitted with a double chimney in October 1957. *P. Ransome-Wallis*

Sparrow Hawk spent all of its days allocated to either Gateshead or Heaton. This superb shot shows the locomotive on a Bristol-Newcastle express leaving York, where it would probably have relieved an LMS 'Jubilee'. As is the case with most of his photographs, Eric Treacy did not record the date. *Eric Treacy*

BR No 60019 (LNER No 4464)

Built	Doncaster December 1937 (Works No 1866)
Name	*Bittern*
Numbers	Originally LNER No 4464
	LNER No 19, September 1957 (No 603 allocated but not carried)
	BR No 60019 October 1948
Double chimney fitted	September 1957
Liveries	Originally LNER Garter blue
	Black November 1941
	LNER Garter blue March 1947
	BR blue July 1950
	BR green February 1952
Allocations	Heaton from new
	Gateshead March 1943
	St Margaret's October 1963
	Aberdeen November 1963
Withdrawn	September 1966; preserved by Mr G. S. Drury of York

▼ In the prewar days, when No 4464 *Bittern* was the only member of the class allocated to Heaton shed at Newcastle, it was regularly used on the up 8.15am Newcastle-King's Cross, returning on alternate weekdays on the down 'Flying Scotsman'. Here it is seen on this diagram leaving King's Cross, and passing a Great Northern Atlantic in the yard on 21 February 1939. *E. R. Wethersett / Ian Allan Library*

▲ It is hard to identify *Bittern*'s livery in this picture, but according to the date — 13 August 1949 — it should be Garter blue. In terrible external condition, the locomotive is climbing Cockburnspath at Bridge 125, which had been replaced after the floods in 1948. *E. R. Wethersett / Ian Allan Library*

▲

Generally *Bittern* was seldom in the limelight until it entered preservation, and even then it had very few main-line outings. Its main claim to fame was working the first up 'Talisman' from Newcastle on 17 September 1956.

This picture shows it on Perth shed (but not in steam) on 13 August 1965, no doubt having failed on one of the three-hour Aberdeen-Glasgow expresses. In addition to the BR Class 20 diesel, the tender of Class A2/3 No 60512 *Steady Aim* can just be seen behind the smokebox.

Following withdrawal it was bought by Mr G. S. Drury and kept at York shed, and hauled a few specials until steam was banned from the BR network. It retains its original tender. After 27 years of inactivity, there are hopes that the locomotive may be returned to working order. *Gavin Morrison*

BR No 60020 (LNER No 4465)

Built	Doncaster December 1937 (Works No 1867)
Name	*Guillemot*
Numbers	Originally LNER No 4465
	LNER No 20, September 1946
	(No 604 allocated but not carried)
	BR No 60020 October 1948
Double chimney fitted	November 1957
Liveries	Originally LNER Garter blue
	Black August 1943
	LNER Garter blue December 1946
	BR blue April 1950
	BR green November 1951
Allocations	Gateshead from new
	Heaton November 1944
	Gateshead October 1945
Withdrawn	March 1964; cut up Darlington Works

No 4465 *Guillemot* was sent to Gateshead when new in the Garter blue livery with dark red wheels, and remained allocated to Tyneside depots throughout its life.

In this picture the locomotive is passing through York non-stop on the up 'Flying Scotsman' during February 1950. By now it is numbered 60020 with 'BRITISH RAILWAYS' on the tender — the letters were in 9in silver-white in Gill Sans lettering. *E. D. Ginz*

A superb picture showing No 60020 in fine external condition leaving York on 10 October 1956 with the 'Junior Scotsman' King's Cross-Glasgow. The shed was just to the right of the picture. *Guillemot* was one of the two 'A4s' to retain the lined-up middle cylinder which was reduced from 18½in to 17in until withdrawal, the other being No 60012 *Commonwealth of Australia*. *Eric Treacy*

A very fine picture of No 4467 *Wild Swan* as it leaves King's Cross on the 'Northern Belle', watched by a crowd on the platform end, c1938. This locomotive spent its career shared between King's Cross, Grantham and Doncaster. It did not receive a corridor tender until April 1957. *E. R. Wethersett / Ian Allan Library*

Considering it was ex works in LNER Garter blue livery only two months before this picture was taken, No 21 *Wild Swan* was looking rather dirty as it emerged from Gas Works Tunnel at Belle Isle on 7 June 1947 at the head of the 5.50pm express to Newcastle. *E. R. Wethersett / Ian Allan Library*

Wild Swan in BR green and in its final form is ready to leave Leeds Central with the 12.30 express to King's Cross on 23 March 1961. It was one of six members of the class to be fitted with a spark-arrester between December 1961 and August 1962. Being one of the earlier members of the class to be withdrawn, it was not transferred to Scotland to end its career. *Gavin Morrison*

BR No 60021 (LNER No 4467)

Built	Doncaster February 1938 (Works No 1869)
Name	*Wild Swan*
Numbers	Originally LNER No 4467
	LNER No 21, May 1946
	(No 606 allocated but not carried)
	BR No 60021 September 1948
Double chimney fitted	April 1958
Liveries	Originally LNER Garter blue
	Black April 1942
	LNER Garter blue April 1947
	BR blue March 1950
	BR green August 1951
Allocations	King's Cross from new
	Doncaster May 1939
	King's Cross August 1941
	Grantham October 1943
	King's Cross August 1944
	Grantham March 1948
	King's Cross June 1950
	New England June 1963
Withdrawn	October 1963; cut up Doncaster Works

A fine portrait of *Mallard* in the yard at King's Cross, and probably taken between
March and July 1938. It is looking superb in its Garter blue livery and dark red
wheels. *P. Ransome-Wallis*

No 4468 *Mallard* was the first 'A4' to receive a double chimney from new. Here it is seen heading the up 'Yorkshire Pullman' near Brookman's Park. This locomotive's epic achievement of 3 July 1938, when it broke the world speed record for steam down Stoke Bank, in the capable hands of driver J. Duddington of Doncaster, has been recorded in detail many times before; the outcome was that the record was snatched from the German Federal Railways by 1½ mph. Whilst 126mph is recorded on the plaques fitted to the locomotive by BR in 1948, Sir Nigel Gresley, who had been hoping for 130mph, accepted the figure as only 125mph.

Mallard was not fitted with a corridor tender until March 1948, but retained this until May 1963, allowing it to be a regular performer on non-stop King's Cross-Edinburgh workings in the 1950s and early 1960s. *LNER Press Department / Ian Allan Library*

No 4468 *Mallard* was the last 'A4' to receive a general repair and be painted in plain black, before the decision was taken to repaint the class in LNER Garter blue. Here it is on the 5.30pm King's Cross-Newcastle on 19 May 1945 at Little Wymondly and looking very drab, with only 'NE' on the tender. It received a hand-painted number 22 in September 1946, and it remained black until January 1948. *E. R. Wethersett / Ian Allan Library*

BR No 60022 (LNER No 4468)

Built	Doncaster March 1938
	(Works No 1870)
Name	*Mallard*
Numbers	Originally LNER No 4468
	LNER No 22, September 1946
	(No 607 allocated but not carried)
	BR No 60022 September 1949
Double chimney fitted	From new
Liveries	Originally LNER Garter blue
	Black June 1942
	LNER Garter blue January 1948
	BR blue September 1949
	BR green July 1952
Allocations	Doncaster from new
	Grantham October 1943
	King's Cross April 1948
Withdrawn	April 1963; preserved at the
	National Railway Museum, York

◄ In January 1948 *Mallard* emerged from Doncaster Works in Garter blue livery with metal cabside numbers (the buffer-beam displaying 'E22'), but with 'BRITISH RAILWAYS' on the tender. It is seen in this livery at the head of the down 'Yorkshire Pullman' at Marshmoor on 14 April 1949. *E. R. Wethersett / Ian Allan Library*

▼ *Mallard* in BR Brunswick green at the head of the down 'Tees-Tyne Pullman' in the 1950s.

The locomotive worked many specials before withdrawal, but one of the earlier ones was on 12 June 1960 from Alford in Lincolnshire to Edinburgh via the Settle & Carlisle and Waverley routes. Another was a 'Northern Rubber' special, via the Calder Valley to Blackpool. When the new diesels were giving trouble in the early 1960s, *Mallard* had during the week ending 2 April 1960 made seven return trips from King's Cross to Newcastle, covering 3,752 miles. It was selected to work the last down 'Elizabethan' in December 1961. After withdrawal it went to Doncaster Works for attention, and emerged externally in its original condition. It was taken to Nine Elms depot at the end of February 1963, and then by road to the Clapham Railway Museum. Its subsequently moved to the National Railway Museum at York, and returned to steam for the 50th anniversary of its record-breaking run. *E. R. Wethersett / Ian Allan Library*

This is an LNER official picture. No 4482 *Golden Eagle* was the first of the second batch of 'A4s', after the four 'Silver' locomotives, to be built. As these locomotives were intended for normal passenger trains, it was decided to paint them in LNER green which matched the 'teak' stock perfectly. Only nine members of the class received the green livery, which was short-lived, as the decision was later taken to adopt the Garter blue as standard. *LNER / Ian Allan Library*

No 4482 *Golden Eagle* must have made a fine sight at the head of the up 'Flying Scotsman' as it passed Marshmoor with a full rake of teak coaches on 25 May 1937. *E. R. Wethersett / Ian Allan Library*

BR No 60023 (LNER No 4482)

Built	Doncaster December 1936
	(Works No 1847)
Name	*Golden Eagle*
Numbers	Originally LNER No 4482
	LNER No 23, November 1946
	(No 584 allocated but not carried)
	BR No 60023 March 1948
Double chimney fitted	September 1958
Liveries	Originally LNER apple green
	LNER Garter blue January 1938
	Black September 1943
	LNER Garter blue
	September 1946
	BR blue August 1949
	BR green September 1952
Allocations	King's Cross from new
	Haymarket February 1938
	Heaton August 1941
	Gateshead January 1942
	St Margaret's October 1963
	Aberdeen May 1964
Withdrawn	October 1964; cut up Motherwell
	Machinery & Scrap Co at Wishaw

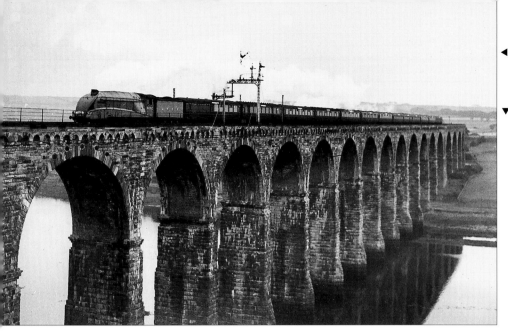

In January 1938 *Golden Eagle* emerged from Doncaster Works in Garter blue, and is shown in this livery at the head of the down 'Flying Scotsman', crossing the Royal Border Bridge at Berwick-on-Tweed on 22 August 1939. *E. R. Wethersett / Ian Allan Library*

Not looking in the best of external condition, No 60023 is shown dead on Gateshead shed, having been ousted from its regular duties by 'Deltics' and other diesels, on 2 August 1961. It lasted another three years, however, being transferred to Scotland, initially to store at Bathgate, and then in traffic at Aberdeen Ferryhill. *Gavin Morrison*

This undated picture of No 4483 *Kingfisher* in LNER green must have been taken in 1937, as it only retained that livery for one year; the location is believed to be Haymarket.

After the war, this locomotive was one of the few Class A4s to receive its allocated number (585) under the LNER's abortive renumbering scheme of January 1946. It was also one of four members of the class to receive the BR lined purple livery, being painted in June 1948 and retaining this for just over two years. It was attached to a corridor tender until August 1966, which allowed it to be a fairly regular performer on the non-stop Edinburgh-King's Cross services whilst allocated to Haymarket. *Ian Allan Library*

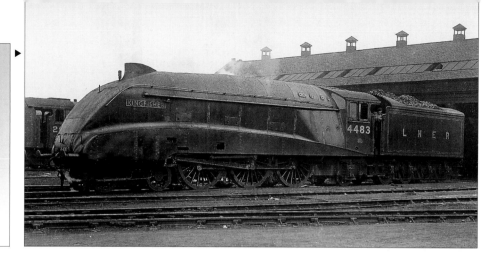

BR No 60024 (LNER No 4483)

Built	Doncaster December 1936 (Works No 1848)
Name	*Kingfisher*
Numbers	Originally LNER No 4483
	LNER No 585 March 1946
	LNER No 24, May 1946
	BR No 60024 June 1948
Double chimney fitted	August 1958
Liveries	Originally LNER apple green
	LNER Garter blue January 1938
	Black February 1943
	LNER Garter blue August 1946
	BR purple June 1948
	BR blue August 1950
	BR green March 1952
Allocations	Haymarket from new
	King's Cross July 1937
	Haymarket January 1938
	Doncaster April 1939
	Haymarket May 1939
	Dalry Road September 1963
	St Margaret's December 1963
	Aberdeen April 1966
Withdrawn	September 1966; cut up by Hughes at Blyth

After its duties on the East Coast main line finished in 1963, *Kingfisher* went first to Dalry Road and then to St Margaret's, before moving to Aberdeen Ferryhill. This transfer is recorded as being in April 1966, but this picture, taken at Stirling on a very wet 14 August 1965, shows a '61B' (Ferryhill) shedplate. The kingfisher plaque, which it received on 21 October 1954 and which was fitted at Haymarket, can be seen on the boiler casing. The train is the 5.30pm Glasgow Buchanan Street-Aberdeen. *Gavin Morrison*

BR No 60025 (LNER No 4484)

Built	Doncaster February 1937 (Works No 1849)
Name	*Falcon*
Numbers	Originally LNER No 4484
	LNER No 25, May 1946 (No 586 believed allocated but not carried)
	BR No 60025 January 1950
Double chimney fitted	September 1958
Liveries	Originally LNER apple green
	LNER Garter blue December 1937
	Black November 1941
	LNER Garter blue December 1947
	BR blue January 1950
	BR green December 1952
Allocations	Haymarket from new
	King's Cross March 1939
	Grantham April 1948
	King's Cross March 1950
	Grantham April 1950
	King's Cross May 1950
	New England June 1963
Withdrawn	October 1963; cut up Doncaster Works

▲ Looking surprisingly clean in its wartime black livery, No 4484 *Falcon* heads an up empty stock working away from Cambridge near Shepreth on 31 July 1943. Whilst it received black livery in November 1941, it was only after July 1942 that the 'NE' letters were applied to the tender, which suggests the locomotive was probably just out of Doncaster Works. It was one of the members of the class always to run with a corridor tender, and was the first of the 'A4s' to lose the front guard irons in December 1952, resulting in the shortening of the cylinder drainpipes. *E. R. Wethersett / Ian Allan Library*

◄ A classic study of *Falcon* in immaculate condition leaving King's Cross at the head of the 'Flying Scotsman', on the centenary of the opening of the Great Northern line, 7 August 1959. *Falcon* hauled the first down 'Talisman' on 17 September 1956, and was one of six 'A4s' to be fitted with a spark-arrester between December 1961 and August 1962. *E. R. Wethersett / Ian Allan Library*

No 4485 *Kestrel*, which became *Miles Beevor* in November 1947, was the most widely allocated member of the class, spending some time at all the sheds in both England and Scotland which over the years had 'A4s' allocated, except Heaton. Here it is seen on the up 'Flying Scotsman' passing Potters Bar in 1937, with the black smokebox sides which were applied to five of the apple green locomotives. *P. Ransome-Wallis*

Kestrel was repainted into LNER Garter blue livery in December 1937. In this picture it is at the head of a down express ready to leave Newcastle Central during 1938. *R. E. Kirkbright*

BR No 60026 (LNER No 4485)

Built	Doncaster February 1937 (Works No 1850)
Names	Originally *Kestrel*; renamed *Miles Beevor* November 1947
Numbers	Originally LNER No 4485
	LNER No 587 April 1946
	LNER No 26, May 1946
	BR No 60026 September 1949
Double chimney fitted	August 1957
Liveries	Originally LNER apple green
	LNER Garter blue
	December 1937
	Black January 1942
	LNER Garter blue
	November 1947
	BR blue September 1949
	BR green January 1953
Allocations	Haymarket February 1937
	Gateshead September 1937
	Haymarket January 1938
	King's Cross March 1939
	Doncaster October 1947
	King's Cross November 1947
	Grantham April 1948
	King's Cross September 1951
	New England June 1963
	St Margaret's October 1963
	Aberdeen April 1964
Withdrawn	December 1965; cut up Hughes at Blyth

In immaculate external condition, and now in BR green livery (it was the last to receive BR green, in January 1953), No 60026 *Miles Beevor* makes a superb sight at the head of the down 'Tees-Tyne Pullman' as it emerges from Gasworks Tunnel. The picture is undated but must have been taken after August 1957, when it received its double chimney. Note the height of the coal in the tender.
Eric Treacy /
Ian Allan Library

BR No 60027 (LNER No 4486)

Built	Doncaster March 1937 (Works No 1851)
Name	*Merlin*
Numbers	Originally LNER No 4486
	LNER No 588 March 1946
	LNER No 27, May 1946
	BR No 60027 June 1948

Double chimney fitted	February 1958	**Allocations**	Haymarket from new
Liveries	Originally LNER apple green		St Rollox May 1962
	LNER Garter blue December 1937		St Margaret's September 1964
	Black December 1941	**Withdrawn**	September 1965; cut up
	LNER Garter blue January 1947		George H. Campbell at Shieldhall
	BR purple June 1948		
	BR blue July 1950		
	BR green June 1952		
	(yellow stripe on cabside c1964)		

◄ *Merlin* went new to Haymarket shed in LNER green livery, and remained on the allocation for over 25 years without being transferred. It changed to a non-corridor tender between March 1948 and July 1948, but then received a corridor type again, which allowed it to be a very regular performer on the non-stop expresses between the two capitals in the 1950s and 1960s. Whilst it remained at Haymarket, it received all the different liveries carried by the class, except grey, as well as its number (588) allocated under the LNER's January 1946 renumbering. It was photographed in August 1937, looking extremely dirty for a Haymarket Pacific, heading an up express across the Forth Bridge. This picture came from the LNER's Public Relations & Publicity Department, which is a surprise, considering the locomotive's external condition. It is still in LNER green with the ugly black-painted smokebox, carried back as far as the first band on the casing.
E. R. Wethersett / Ian Allan Library

This picture, by contrast to the previous one, shows *Merlin* as BR No 60027, in the external condition normally associated with the famous Haymarket 'A4s'. It is at the head of the up 'Elizabethan' near Woolmer Green on 11 July 1958. Note the plaque on the boiler casing, which had originally been fitted on the cabside. In the summer of 1960 *Merlin* was the main Haymarket performer on the 'Elizabethan', hauling 74 trains, 46 of which were consecutive between 22 June and 6 August, so the class's prewar achievements were being repeated 22 years later, in the postwar era. In May 1962 *Merlin* was transferred to St Rollox shed, where the 'A4s' were not favourably received by most of the men, and on 22 February 1962 was used on a test train for the three-hour Aberdeen expresses. Towards the end of its life it was one of two of the class to receive the diagonal yellow cabside stripe, prohibiting its use under overhead electrification south of Crewe. It ended its days at St Margaret's, only a few miles from Haymarket. *E. R. Wethersett / Ian Allan Library*

◄ *Sea Eagle* was another member of the class to carry all the liveries, except grey. This picture, taken at King's Cross in 1937 when the locomotive was almost new, shows the black skirting and the black smokebox painted to the first boiler band casing, which gives a very odd appearance. It was one of five to receive this treatment, but ran thus only for a short period. *D. W. Allen*

BR No 60028 (LNER No 4487)

Built	Doncaster April 1937 (Works No 1852)
Names	Originally *Sea Eagle*; renamed *Walter K. Whigham* October 1947
Numbers	Originally LNER No 4487
	LNER No 28, November 1946 (No 589 allocated but not carried)
	BR No 60028 June 1948
Double chimney fitted	November 1957
Liveries	Originally LNER apple green
	LNER Garter blue February 1938
	Black November 1941
	LNER Garter blue October 1947
	BR purple June 1948
	BR blue October 1950
	BR green February 1952

Allocations
Gateshead from new
Haymarket February 1938
Doncaster March 1939
Haymarket April 1939
King's Cross May 1939
Grantham October 1945
King's Cross May 1948.

Withdrawn December 1962; cut up Doncaster Works

Now in LNER blue livery, No 4487 *Sea Eagle* makes an impressive sight as it storms up the 1 in 190 bank out of Berwick-upon-Tweed to Burnmouth on the down 'Flying Scotsman', having covered over 340 miles of the 392½-mile journey, in August 1939. It became one of the first in the class to lose the skirting over the wheels, in July 1941. *E. R. Wethersett / Ian Allan Library*

In October 1947 *Sea Eagle* became *Walter K. Whigham*. Two months before receiving its double chimney in November 1957, it is seen passing St Neots at the head of the down 3.40 King's Cross-Niddrie goods, which was often hauled by 'A4s' around this period.

In the hands of Haymarket driver W. Stevenson, No 60028 *Walter K. Whigham* was the first locomotive to achieve the British record for non-stop steam haulage of 408.65 miles, when on 24 August 1948 it hauled the up 'Flying Scotsman' via the Waverley Route to St Boswells, then via Kelso and Tweedmouth to join the ECML, due to flooding around Cockburnspath. This diversion was repeated on a further 16 occasions that year, eight in each direction. No 60028 also hauled the first down 'Elizabethan' in 1953, and, complete with white cab roof, worked one of the Royal specials to York for HRH The Duke of Kent's wedding on 8 June 1961. *E. R. Wethersett / Ian Allan Library*

BR No 60029 (LNER No 4493)

Built	Doncaster July 1937 (Works No 1858)
Name	*Woodcock*
Numbers	Originally LNER No 4493
	LNER No 29, May 1946 (No 595 allocated but not carried)
	BR No 60029 July 1948
Double chimney fitted	October 1958
Liveries	Originally LNER apple green
	LNER Garter blue July 1938
	Black September 1942
	LNER Garter blue June 1947
	BR purple July 1948
	BR blue January 1950
	BR green October 1952
Allocations	Gateshead from new
	Doncaster January 1938
	King's Cross February 1938
	Gateshead August 1943
	King's Cross October 1943
	New England June 1963
Withdrawn	October 1963; cut up Doncaster Works

▼ Two months after exchanging apple green for the Garter blue, No 4493 *Woodcock* bursts out of one of the Welwyn tunnels at the head of the then Saturday-only 8.55am Glasgow Queen Street-King's Cross on 17 September 1938. This locomotive received all the different liveries, except the grey/silver. It moved between the English depots until 1943, when it settled at King's Cross for 20 years. *E. R. Wethersett / Ian Allan Library*

▲ On 20 April 1946 *Woodcock* was still in wartime black with only 'NE' on the tender. It is passing New Southgate at the head of the 4pm King's Cross-Leeds. *E. R. Wethersett / Ian Allan Library*

Woodcock has now changed its number to 29, and received the Garter blue livery one month before this picture was taken on 5 July 1947; its external condition would suggest it had not been cleaned since it left the works. It is heading a down express past New Southgate. *E. R. Wethersett / Ian Allan Library*

What a fine sight *Woodcock* (now No 60029) must have made at the head of the down 'Yorkshire Pullman' in the short-lived BR lined purple livery. One of four 'A4s' to receive this livery, it is seen passing Marshmoor on 25 May 1949. *E. R. Wethersett / Ian Allan Library*

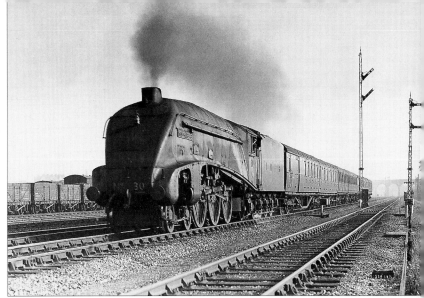

BR No 60030 (LNER No 4495)

Built	Doncaster August 1937 (Works No 1860)
Names	Originally *Great Snipe*; renamed *Golden Fleece* September 1937
Numbers	Originally LNER No 4495
	LNER No 30, November 1946 (No 597 allocated but not carried)
	BR No 60030 July 1948
Double chimney fitted	May 1958
Liveries	Originally LNER apple green
	LNER Garter blue September 1937
	Black December 1941
	LNER Garter blue December 1946
	BR blue November 1949
	BR green September 1952
Allocations	Doncaster from new
	King's Cross September 1937
	Grantham December 1939
	King's Cross July 1942
	Grantham October 1942
	King's Cross June 1950
	Grantham April 1957
	King's Cross September 1957
Withdrawn	December 1962; cut up Doncaster Works

▼ No 4495 *Golden Fleece* was originally painted green, but was then selected for the 'West Riding Limited', so returned to Doncaster after two weeks and re-emerged in Garter blue. In 1939 it worked the streamlined train for 14 consecutive weeks, with only three days off. In all it hauled 258 of the 968 'West Riding' trains. The locomotive is seen here on 11 June 1938 at Woolmer Green, having a day off from its regular duty with a Leeds-King's Cross train. It carried the name *Great Snipe* for only one month, receiving *Golden Fleece* in September 1937. *E. R. Wethersett / Ian Allan Library*

▲ Now No 30, and having regained Garter blue livery after five years in wartime black, *Golden Fleece* heads a down slow Cambridge train near New Southgate on 6 October 1947. Note the articulated suburban coaches next to the locomotive. *E. R. Wethersett / Ian Allan Library*

◄ A fine study of 60030 *Golden Fleece* ready to leave King's Cross. During the early main-line diesel days, *Golden Fleece* ran no less than 9,018 miles on a daily diagram of the 10.00 down 'Flying Scotsman' as far as Newcastle, returning to King's Cross with an express at 5pm. This feat was achieved between 30 November and 20 December 1958. *Ian Allan Library*

▼ With coal stacked above the height of the cab, *Golden Fleece*, now in final condition, heads north past Stukeley on 11 September 1959 at the head of the 3.40pm King's Cross-Niddrie goods, on which the 'A4s' were regularly diagrammed at this time. *E. R. Wethersett / Ian Allan Library*

BR No 60031 (LNER No 4497)

Built	Doncaster October 1937 (Works No 1862)
Name	*Golden Plover*
Numbers	Originally LNER No 4497
	LNER No 31, May 1946
	(No 599 allocated but not carried)
	BR No 60031 June 1948
Double chimney fitted	March 1958
Liveries	Originally LNER Garter blue
	Black May 1942
	LNER Garter blue August 1947
	BR blue July 1949
	BR green July 1952
	(yellow stripe on cabside c1964)
Allocations	Haymarket from new
	St Rollox February 1962
Withdrawn	October 1965; cut up George H. Campbell at Shieldhall

Golden Plover, originally numbered 4497, went new in Garter blue livery to Haymarket, where it stayed for 25 years until steam finished on East Coast main line expresses. It was a regular performer on the 'Coronation', and in the spring of 1939 made 31 consecutive trips, covering 15,327 miles in six weeks. In total it hauled 125 of the 1,084 'Coronations'.

It will be noticed that *Golden Plover* was running without a tender emblem when this photograph was taken on 6 August 1949. *Union of South Africa* also ran thus at this time, both locomotives then being in BR blue livery. *Golden Plover* was always attached to a corridor tender, so was a frequent performer on the 'Capitals' and 'Elizabethan' expresses. *E. R. Wethersett / Ian Allan Library*

In February 1962 *Golden Plover* was transferred to Glasgow St Rollox, where apparently it and the other 'A4s' were not well received by the majority of the crews. It tended to work the Dundee trains rather than the three-hour Aberdeen expresses, which were in the hands of the Ferryhill 'A4s'. As can be seen, *Golden Plover* was one of two members of the class to have the diagonal yellow cabside stripe barring it from working south of Crewe, which would have been highly unlikely in any case. It is shown leaving Perth at the head of a Dundee-Glasgow Buchanan Street train in terrible external condition on 14 August 1965. *Gavin Morrison*

No 4900 *Gannet* storms through the north London suburbs on a down express prior to its September 1942 repaint into wartime black livery. *Ian Allan Library*

In BR days as No 60032, *Gannet* hauls an afternoon Leeds-King's Cross past Holbeck High Level. The photographer has obviously asked the crew to organise some exhaust, as they are having a look out of the cab to make sure their efforts are being recorded. The locomotive later became the last 'A4' to receive a double chimney, in November 1958, and was one of six to be fitted with a spark-arrester between December 1961 and August 1962. It covered 1,351,887 miles in service — the lowest mileage for any member of the class. *Ian Allan Library*

BR No 60032 (LNER No 4900)

Built	Doncaster May 1938 (Works No 1874)
Name	*Gannet*
Numbers	Originally LNER No 4900
	LNER No 32, November 1946
	(No 610 allocated but not carried)
	BR No 60032 June 1949
Double chimney fitted	November 1958
Liveries	Originally LNER Garter blue
	Black September 1942
	LNER Garter blue May 1947
	BR blue June 1949
	BR green October 1952
Allocations	Doncaster from new
	Grantham September 1938
	King's Cross September 1938
	Doncaster May 1939
	Grantham October 1943
	King's Cross June 1950
	New England June 1963
Withdrawn	October 1963; cut up

Seagull was one of the four 'A4s' to be built with a double chimney. Here it is seen in its original condition numbered 4902 and fitted with a non-corridor tender, at the head of the 4pm King's Cross-Leeds near Sandy on 28 August 1938, when only two months old. *E. R. Wethersett / Ian Allan Library*

By now BR No 60033, *Seagull* climbs Stoke Bank with apparent ease at the head of a King's Cross-Leeds express on 21 July 1962. Notice the state of the embankments: not a bush in sight; one wonders what they are like today. The locomotive received a corridor tender in April 1948, which allowed it to be used on the non-stop trains to Edinburgh on a regular basis. It took part in the 1948 locomotive exchanges with the Western Region and performed very well indeed, having substituted for *Mallard,* which failed on 28 April 1948. *Gavin Morrison*

BR No 60033 (LNER No 4902)

Built	Doncaster June 1938 (Works No 1876)
Name	*Seagull*
Numbers	Originally LNER No 4902
	LNER No 33, October 1946
	(No 612 allocated but not carried)
	BR No 60033 April 1948
Double chimney fitted	From new
Liveries	Originally LNER Garter blue
	Black May 1942
	LNER Garter blue
	December 1947
	BR blue November 1950
	BR green June 1952
Allocations	King's Cross from new
	Grantham April 1944
	King's Cross March 1948
Withdrawn	December 1962; cut up
	Doncaster Works

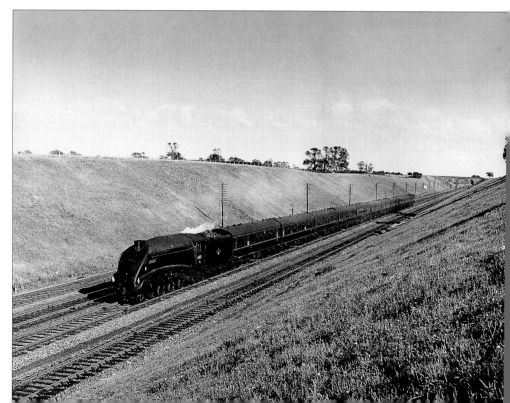

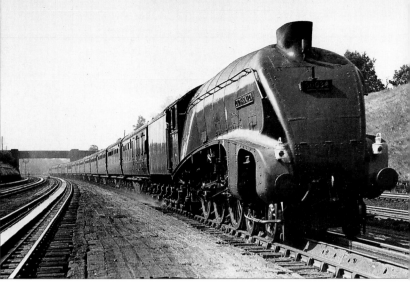

Peregrine was the last 'A4' to be built, and emerged from Doncaster Works in July 1938. it is shown passing New Southgate when only three months old at the head of the 4pm King's Cross-Leeds. Note the fine Great Northern somersault signals.

The locomotive was renamed *Lord Faringdon* in March 1948. It was originally fitted with a streamlined non-corridor tender, but exchanged it for a corridor version in February 1948, which it retained until January 1963. It is recorded as being the only 'A4' never to work one of the streamlined express trains, but had the distinction of working the first down postwar 'Flying Scotsman'. *E. R. Wethersett / Ian Allan Library*

No 60034 *Lord Faringdon* was the last 'A4' to retain LNER Garter blue livery, although it received the number 60034 and 'BRITISH RAILWAYS' on the tender in March 1948. It was selected to take part in the 1948 locomotive exchanges, as it had covered the correct mileage since its last visit to works. Having taken part in the trials between King's Cross and Leeds in April, it worked the 'Royal Scot' on the West Coast main line between Euston and Carlisle, and is shown at the head of the up train on Bushey troughs on 17 May 1948. Thereafter it spent its days at King's Cross before having a final fling on the Glasgow-Aberdeen three-hour expresses. *E. R. Wethersett / Ian Allan Library*

BR No 60034 (LNER No 4903)

Built	Doncaster July 1938 (Works No 1877)
Names	Originally *Peregrine*; renamed *Lord Faringdon* March 1948
Numbers	Originally LNER No 4903
	LNER No 34, November 1946 (No 613 allocated but not carried)
	BR No 60034 March 1948
Double chimney fitted	From new
Liveries	Originally LNER Garter blue
	Black September 1942
	LNER Garter blue December 1947
	BR blue December 1950
	BR green August 1952
Allocations	Doncaster from new
	King's Cross July 1942
	Grantham October 1942
	King's Cross April 1948
	New England June 1963
	St Margaret's October 1963
	Aberdeen May 1964
Withdrawn	August 1966; cut up Hughes at Blyth

Having worked a Sunday morning King's Cross-Leeds express, No 60007 *Sir Nigel Gresley* pauses at Leeds Central station prior to backing up to Copley Hill shed for servicing, on 28 February 1960. The picture clearly shows the corridor tender. *Gavin Morrison*

No 60025 *Falcon*, in customary immaculate 'Top Shed' condition, approaches Great Ponton with an up express on 27 August 1960. *Gavin Morrison*

Haymarket's No 60011 *Empire of India* stands at Doncaster shed following a visit to the works on 6 November 1960. *Gavin Morrison*

In fine external condition, Top Shed's No 60025 *Falcon* prepares to leave Leeds Central with the 12.30 to King's Cross on 24 April 1961. *Gavin Morrison*

The down 'Talisman' nears the end of its journey, passing Drem on 14 July 1961. No 60001 *Sir Ronald Matthews* is in charge, and is in poor external condition — not uncommon for Gateshead Pacifics at this time. *Gavin Morrison*

No 60016 *Silver King* at its home depot of Gateshead, with 'cod's mouth' open for servicing, on 2 August 1961. *Gavin Morrison*

The up 'Heart of Midlothian' passes Tollerton in the Vale of York on a fine summer's afternoon, 6 August 1961. It is a pity that the external condition of Gateshead's No 60020 *Guillemot* does not match that of the 12 maroon coaches. *Gavin Morrison*

No 60033 *Seagull*, not in the usual 'Top Shed' condition, awaits its next duty back to King's Cross at Copley Hill shed on 23 October 1961. *Gavin Morrison*

Haymarket's No 60011 *Empire of India* makes a very rare appearance at Leeds Holbeck shed on 26 February 1962. It is believed to have worked the Edinburgh Waverley-London St Pancras sleeper, standing in for a failed 'Peak' class diesel-electric. It is in terrible external condition for a Haymarket Pacific, and was transferred to Aberdeen Ferryhill three months later. *Gavin Morrison*

No 60007 *Sir Nigel Gresley* makes a dramatic departure from Leeds central past Copley Hill shed at the head of the up 'Yorkshire Pullman' on 12 March 1962. *Gavin Morrison*

A dirty No 60003 *Andrew K. McCosh* storms past Beeston junction on the outskirts of Leeds at the head of the up 'Yorkshire Pullman' on 14 March 1962. By this date it was very likely to have been covering for a failed diesel locomotive. *Gavin Morrison*

No 60030 *Golden Fleece* makes a dramatic climb out of Leeds past Copley Hill shed on the 10am Leeds Central-King's Cross on 9 April 1962. *Gavin Morrison*

Another view of *Sir Nigel Gresley*, passing Beeston Junction on the outskirts of Leeds on the 10.00 Leeds Central-King's Cross on 12 April 1962. *Gavin Morrison*

No 60017 *Silver Fox* on Doncaster shed (36A) on the afternoon of 29 April 1962, being prepared to take over an express to King's Cross at later in the day. The stainless steel fox emblem can be clearly seen on the boiler casing. *Gavin Morrison*

After being prepared on Doncaster shed, No 60017 makes an impressive sight as it leaves Doncaster station with an express for King's Cross on 29 April 1962. *Gavin Morrison*

A line-up of locomotives on Doncaster shed awaiting a visit to 'The Plant' on 29 April 1962. From left to right are Grantham's Class A3 No 60106 *Flying Fox*, 'A4' No 60021 *Wild Swan* from King's Cross and 'Britannia' No 70011 *Hotspur*, which was allocated to March shed. This may well have been *Wild Swan*'s last visit to the works. *Gavin Morrison*

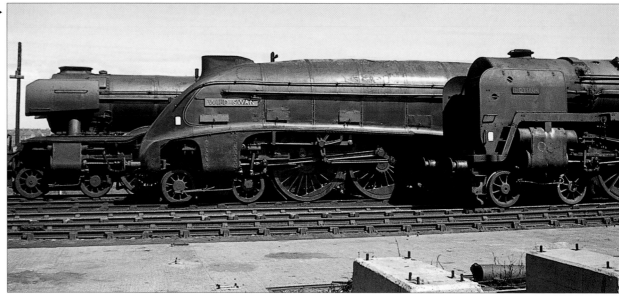

In 1962 the 10.00 from Leeds Central to King's Cross was frequently hauled by a 'Top Shed' 'A4'. On 5 June 1962 No 60033 *Seagull*, one of the original trio of double-chimney members of the class allocated to King's Cross (34A), makes a fine sight passing the signalbox at Beeston Junction as it climbs towards Ardsley Tunnel on its journey south. *Gavin Morrison*

No 60011 *Empire of India*, allocated to Haymarket, pulls away from Holbeck High Level, Leeds, on the 5.15pm stopping train to Doncaster. This was often used around this time as a running-in turn for Pacifics which had just received general overhauls at Doncaster Works. The date was 5 June 1962, so it is likely this was the locomotive's last major repair. *Gavin Morrison*

On two consecutive days in June 1962, there were ex-works 'A4s' running-in on the all-stations 5.15pm Leeds-Doncaster local. No 60034 *Lord Faringdon* makes easy work of the lightweight train, which had an articulated set of coaches at the front. It is passing Beeston Junction, on the outskirts of Leeds, on 6 June 1962. *Gavin Morrison*

King's Cross's No 60032 *Gannet* heads north through the Vale of York near Benningborough on a down express as a freight passes on the up slow line, on 16 June 1962. *Gavin Morrison*

This is one of the plaques attached to *Mallard* to commemorate its world speed record, although they were not fitted to the locomotive until 1948, 10 years after the historic event. The plaques show 126mph, but it is reported that Sir Nigel Gresley himself believed it should be 125mph. *Gavin Morrison*

▲

The fire in No 60001 *Sir Ronald Matthews* does not seem to be in very good condition as the locomotive approaches Stoke Tunnel after a long climb up the bank, on a down freight on 7 July 1962. *Gavin Morrison*

On 29 September 1962 — a fine, hot day — King's Cross's No 60013 *Dominion of New Zealand* heads south past Benningborough without a hint of exhaust.
Gavin Morrison

The Town Hall is just visible in the background as King's Cross's No 60030 *Golden Fleece* climbs out of Leeds Central past Holbeck High Level with the 12.55 express to King's Cross. This locomotive was one of the first to be withdrawn, two months after this picture was taken on 4 October 1962. *Gavin Morrison*

The up 'White Rose' (minus headboard) passes over the former LNWR goods yards at Wortley South Junction, Leeds, headed by a well-cleaned King's Cross 'A4', No 60017 *Silver Fox*, on 5 October 1963. *Gavin Morrison*

The nameplates fitted to *Silver Link* and *Quicksilver* had rounded corners as illustrated, whereas those on the rest of the class had square corners. *Silver Link* was one of the first four of the class to be withdrawn, in December 1962, and three months later the nameplates were still in place, the locomotive having been dumped in the works yard at Doncaster. *Gavin Morrison*

Still looking in reasonable external condition, in spite of having been withdrawn four months previously, No 60014 *Silver Link* stands in Doncaster Works yard, awaiting a private buyer that sadly never came. Surely this locomotive was worthy of preservation. *Gavin Morrison*

▲

No 60022 *Mallard* in clean condition at Doncaster shed on 3 March 1963 — only one
month before its withdrawal for preservation. *Gavin Morrison*

This was probably the last occasion that an 'A4' worked up to King's Cross from Leeds Central. The days of immaculate Pacifics at Top Shed had passed, and No 60025 *Falcon* made a depressing sight as it prepared to leave Leeds Central on the last steam-worked 'White Rose', on 15 June 1963. The locomotive was withdrawn four months later. *Gavin Morrison*

A fireman's view of an 'A4' Pacific — in this case No 60023 *Golden Eagle* — as it approaches Ribblehead Viaduct on a dismal 30 June 1963 at the head of a West Riding Railway Correspondence & Travel Society special to Scotland. The locomotive achieved an average of 78.4mph for the 40.9 miles between Mallerstang signalbox and Cumwhinton; the maximum speed attained over this stretch was 93mph. *Gavin Morrison*

Once the pride of Gateshead shed, No 60016 *Silver King* presents a sorry sight on a very rare visit to Leeds Holbeck shed on 23 September 1963. One month later it was transferred to St Margaret's, Edinburgh, and two weeks after that to Aberdeen Ferryhill to work the Glasgow-Aberdeen three-hour expresses. *Gavin Morrison*

Ironically it was Haymarket's most famous 'A4' that hauled the last British Railways steam special from King's Cross to Newcastle, on 24 October 1964. The train, named the 'Jubilee Requiem', was organised by the Railway Correspondence & Travel Society and the Stephenson Locomotive Society. In this view No 60009 *Union of South Africa* receives attention at Gateshead shed prior to the return working. The locomotive gave a good performance, but did not reach the magic 'ton'. *Gavin Morrison*

Probably the most famous of all Haymarket's Class A4 Pacifics, No 60009 *Union of South Africa* enjoyed a final fling on the Glasgow-Aberdeen expresses. It is seen at the north end of Perth station, ready to depart for Aberdeen on 13 August 1965. *Gavin Morrison*

On 19 September 1965 the West Riding Branch of the Railway Correspondence & Travel Society ran a special to the North East from Leeds. 'A4' No 60004 *William Whitelaw* was despatched from Aberdeen Ferryhill to work the trains, and is seen here at Eaglescliffe. *Gavin Morrison*

Sir Nigel Gresley's first outing in preservation, following overhaul at Crewe Works, was over Shap and Ais Gill summits on 1 April 1967. On 20 August 1967 it was out on the East Coast main line again, and is shown approaching York, past the old racecourse station, with a special for Edinburgh Waverley. *Gavin Morrison*

This picture shows the two apertures of the Kylchap double chimney, and the small holes to the rear for ventilating the sniffing or anti-vacuum valve. The chimney casing was made of copper sheeting to prevent corrosion, and the liners of cast iron. The picture is of No 60009 *Union of South Africa*, and was taken from the top of the retaining wall at Dundee station on 8 September 1973. *Gavin Morrison*

On a glorious late summer's evening, No 60009 *Union of South Africa* leaves Ladybank on on an Edinburgh-Dundee special on 8 September 1973. *Gavin Morrison*

On 22 June 1974, by now preserved in Garter blue, *Sir Nigel Gresley* worked a special from Edinburgh to Aberdeen — believed the furthest north this locomotive has been in preservation. The 'A4s' always attracted the crowds and still do; the stop at Dundee on the return trip was no exception. *Gavin Morrison*

No 60009 *Union of South Africa* makes one of its usual spirited departures from Edinburgh Waverley through Princes Street Gardens, heading for Dundee on the 'Forth & Tay' special on 7 June 1975. 'Deltic' No 55 015 *Tulyar* in the background, heading for the station to work the up 'Flying Scotsman'. Both locomotives are now preserved. *Gavin Morrison*

On the afternoon of Friday 29 April 1977, when No 4498 *Sir Nigel Gresley* was
visiting the National Railway Museum, the opportunity was taken to have a line-up
alongside No 4468 *Mallard*. The two versions of the LNER blue livery on the
locomotives make an interesting comparison. *Gavin Morrison*

Sir Nigel Gresley 'opens up' on the approach to Settle Junction, off the Carnforth line, at the head of the 'North Yorkshireman' special on 29 August 1979. The line to Carlisle can be seen on the right of the picture.
Gavin Morrison

Looking splendid in its BR green livery, No 60009 *Union of South Africa* heads north from Perth on its old stamping-ground on 27 June 1980. This time, however, it is bound not for Aberdeen but for Aviemore, on the 'Royal Highlander' special. This was the first visit of an 'A4' to the Highland main line, and there were many speed restrictions. The locomotive ran light-engine to Inverness to turn on the triangle before returning to Aviemore to work back to Perth. *Gavin Morrison*

Sir Nigel Gresley catches a rare flash of sunlight on a typically stormy day on the
Settle & Carlisle, as it heads north from Ribblehead Viaduct on a Pullman special on
23 November 1981. *Gavin Morrison*

Although No 60009 *Union of South Africa* spent virtually its entire working career allocated to Haymarket, with just a short spell at Aberdeen Ferryhill, since preservation it has been seen all over the country. One of its many trips over the Settle-Carlisle line was on 28 April 1984, when it headed the down 'Cumbrian Mountain Express'. Here it is crossing Smardale Viaduct, the highest viaduct on the line at 130ft, and 237yd long. *Gavin Morrison*

Since the return of steam to the main lines back in October 1971, there have been relatively few specials between Thornhill Junction in West Yorkshire and Leeds via the old London & North Western route, especially in the up direction. *Sir Nigel Gresley* made a rare appearance on 9 June 1984, heading a Clitheroe to York special, and is seen passing Batley Carr. *Gavin Morrison*

During the short period around 1988 when *Mallard* returned to the main line to commemorate the 50 years since its world speed record, it was used on specials. One of these was the 'Pennine Postal', which crossed the Pennines via the Standedge route on its way to York. The train is seen rounding the curve just to the east of Marsden station on 10 May 1988. *Gavin Morrison*

The Railway Correspondence & Travel Society 'Diamond Jubilee' special was hauled by *Mallard*. The special is passing through the impressive Horbury Cutting on the old Lancashire & Yorkshire main line, just to the east of Healey Mills marshalling yard, on 30 July 1988. *Gavin Morrison*

After more than 25 years in preservation, when it had been painted in LNER blue, the 'A4' Locomotive Society, owners of *Sir Nigel Gresley*, decided to repaint the locomotive in the short-lived BR lined blue livery, and numbered 60007. In BR service it only carried this livery between September 1950 and April 1952.

This picture is taken on the Great Central Railway, and shows the locomotive hauling an evening train away from Loughborough at Woodthorpe Lane on 6 November 1994. *Gavin Morrison*

Another view of *Sir Nigel Gresley* in BR blue livery, but this time on the East Lancashire Railway at Irwell Vale station in the winter sunshine on 25 January 1998. *Gavin Morrison*

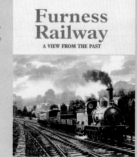

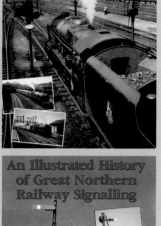